What Business Owners Are Saying About 57 Media Spikes

57 Media Spikes

When I started reading your insider's stuff I thought it was too detailed and too long, the complete opposite to what we're told you're supposed to do with online communications.

But your weird passion for advertising and media, your voice, your personality, is coming through in every piece and the effect grows stronger with each one. What comes through, other than your obvious expertise and experience, is your sincerity.

It's damn near unbelievable that anyone could be as sincere about their work in advertising in this cynical day and age as you are. It's as if I'm reading something stuck for 60 or 70 years in a time warp that is just now reaching its destination. And yet it's current. It's as if Rosser Reeves or Ted Bates has come back from the dead.

By the way, other than you and I, there's no one in the world that remembers Reeves or Bates. Maybe people remember David Ogilvy, another dude who'd heartily agree with you, but I very much doubt it. So keep up the messages, my friend, and I hope they bring you lots of business.

Bruce MacDonald, President, Invisible Hand
www.invisihand.com

57 Media Spikes is the skillful distillation of 30 years of working in the Canadian media world and covers all aspects of old media, new media and everything in between.

In a series of engaging vignettes, Dennis Kelly explains how to construct a successful media strategy no matter what your level of experience in media planning might be, regardless of whether you have a large or small budget.

He clearly lays out the merits and drawbacks of the many media choices available today and explains the necessity of continual testing and fine-tuning a media plan to ensure that it delivers maximum results. "A media plan" he states, "is an ongoing process. It continually changes because the market conditions continually change."

There is also a strong emphasis on managing your own expectations if you handle your own media planning, or managing your clients expectations if you plan for others. While other publications of this type tend to talk of nothing but success, Mr. Kelly is a realist.
"There will be failures " he says, " The key is to recognize them quickly, learn from them and make that experience work for you in the future"

Much of the appeal of 57 Media Spikes comes from the way in which it is written. The style is personal; the information often presented in everyday scenarios that everyone can relate to. It is almost as if you are not reading at all but having a personal conversation with the author.

And this perhaps is the biggest benefit of all from this fine publication.
It draws you in, makes it easy for you to absorb the information and understand how this all helps to make effective day to day media decisions.

It's a guide that every media and marketing professional should have on their desk.

Terry Coster, President, Coster Media
Toronto, Canada

57 Media Spikes

Uncorking The Media Genie

**30 Years of Media Planning and Buying
Secrets
Unbottled At Last**

Dennis W. Kelly
First Impressions Media

Spike of Angels - A Division of First Impressions Media

Table of Contents

Preface

How We Got Here

Education! An ongoing classroom started by real-life experience.

Has this happened to you? Through more presentations than I care to recount, I came away disheartened.

Feeling that gnawing sense of frustration when you think you've done everything right, but couldn't quite close the sale. You were THIS close, you know the feeling I mean, close enough to taste it - already planned how you'd spend the commission close, - and the client paused. Wouldn't sign. 'What if...' hung in the air like an unwelcome odour. He waited. Could not or would not commit.

Beneath a calm veneer my mind is exploding at the boardroom table.... 'C'mon, What are you waiting for – A Streetcar!' Sign the contract!!!

Those soul crushing pauses were the inspiration for the pages you have in front of you right now. I'm Dennis Kelly. I wrote 57 Media Spikes to offer some advertising planning and buying guidance. Before you open your wallet to strangers who want to sell you everything that might sell your something, you'll want to read this.

Just by opening these pages you are leaps and bounds ahead of your competitors. You'll discover insights, strategies, tips and philosophies that will enhance your advertising, teach you something in each media, and improve your media placement and ROI. (Return On Investment – I know you know that abbreviation, but another reader might not.)

You'll reap the benefits of my 30 years of ad planning and buying. Lucky you!

That nervewracking feeling we had in the boardroom, as a client waffles on a decision can weaken the most battle-hardened nerves of steel. Feels familiar doesn't it? Maybe on both sides of the desk this plays out equally.

In examining the presentations that went exceedingly well, where I had the client buy into my recommendation, as compared to the ones that were less successful, I noticed one key trait emerging.

My clients had grown to trust me. Felt confident in my work. I was doing a great job, but once in a while the magic wasn't there for them. Like the above.

I railed- **Why** Don't They Get It? **Why** Don't They Understand What a Great Opportunity This Is? **What's** Missing?

Like an Indiana Jones torch of fire ever so slowly illuminating the deepest caverns with flickering bursts, the realization spread over me and opened my eyes.

They are not saying Yes because you, Dennis, you haven't shown them yet what a great deal it is. YOU Need to be the one to educate them. What was patently obvious to me, ie: that they should take this Outside Back Cover position at a 3x frequency discount, and no premium position charge, was meaningless to them.

They needed to be educated- by me- exactly why these opportunities were such a great deal. Not just for money savings (although that was important).

No it was deeper than that. They needed to understand how this was going to elevate their product to the target group they were after. Being in this media vehicle was going to raise their profile better than any other one because of its unique ability to penetrate all the clutter and deliver the message smack in front of the target groups' eyeballs.

Embracing this thinking, my subsequent presentations went into more details and rationale why this was great fit, what excellent value/ positioning it offered, and why it was part of my recommendation.

Acceptance of my recommendations skyrocketed. Now the client was making a more informed decision. Understanding better what it was they were buying into. Their confidence in me soared, and their spending increased as they felt much more empowered and educated about why they were choosing what they chose.

From that realization came better plans. Better ad campaigns. Better, more efficient media buys. Sounder strategies and media mixes.

This begat my improved campaign development by educating my clients as we went along and not just putting a recommendation out there. Rather, I was explaining to them, as I would to you – on paper and in vocal presentations, why I was presenting what I believed would be the best use of their funds and how it would showcase their creative to best advantage.

So We Got Here...How? In the wake of years of these presentations, I felt compelled to share this to more candidates. I don't delude myself. Media buying isn't rocket science, neurosurgery, nor the Human Genome project calibre work.

But to every client who has opened up a wallet of hard-earned money, they have a right to know their money will be well spent.

Educating as I presented laid the foundations for better campaigns. More informed clients asked better questions. New information from them emerged. They now understood why one tactic was chosen versus another.

I've tried to impart this same thinking into 57 Media Spikes. What you are holding is the refinement of 30 years of media planning and buying for large and small clients in large and small ad agencies. This began life as a brief, one time explanation. More stories, and education ultimately expanded to an e-mail series via my website (firstimpressionsmedia.ca).

It has emerged as the desktop Media Director you have in hand.

Some of these tips will be 'Spot-On' for you. That's perfect.
Some others may seem 'quaint', or less relevant to you. That's fine too.

You are coming to these pages from multiple sources, experiences and background. As such, I allowed some latitude in the content to ensure
all my readers' common interests in media are highlighted with selective gems that speak to them with exactly the direction they need.

Consider it a Recipe book if you will. All related to media, but all with differing tastes.

Strategies, philosophies, and tips across all media to help you become an even sharper customer. When you can come to the table with a better understanding of media costs, demands, and what each one can or can't do, you are a better client to work with. Expectations can be better managed, and the value delivered by your media team appreciated all the more.

I'm glad you're here. Let's get started.

Media Spike #1 – Get It Right The First Time

Welcome,

The most amazing part of your advertising is the endless opportunities you have to announce **YOU ARE HERE!**

As we kick-off our series, I want you to always remember each media you choose is your platform.

You have command of the floor, the stage, the spotlight and it's your chance to shine. That product or service on profile is the embodiment of everything you are. And it's on display for everyone you target to see.

Let's make sure you always give yourself the chance to look your very best.

This week's ad of yours may be the only piece, yes, the only piece a candidate buyer ever sees or hears of you.

We hope there's more, BUT, it may be the one time they get to see you and absorb your message.

There will never be a second chance to make a good First Impression.

Don't _ever_ give away a time at bat.

Make sure the first time you're out there, the 33rd time, the 116th time, you look exactly the way you want to be remembered.

That ad may be the only sliver of content, or image, anyone sees of you.
Think of how you want to be recollected. Get it right the first time.

Ah but Dennis, you may whine, I don't have that kind of time to get it right.
It might not be unfamiliar to you to hear someone vent to the effect,
Why is there never enough time to do it right the first time, but there's always plenty of time to do it over again?

You've heard that too? Maybe said it yourself? Me too.

And it's troubling when we are suddenly pressured to compose a week's work into a frenzied afternoon to make the proposal ready. Time is of the essence. Deliver it, and when it's at last reviewed 3 days later, a host of changes arise.

You then spend a week making all the client requested changes which would not have been necessary if you had had the time to plan it properly in the first place.

That's why I harken back to the importance of making a good first impression. It can't be undone, and if it's done well, it won't need to be.

If done smartly, it can pave the way for a wonderful relationship with your friends, partner, sibling, employer, and client. Critically, once nurtured, a good impression gains you an indulgence bank. Every once in a while you'll have a hiccup. You know the ones I'm talking about.

The day that everything that could go wrong...did. But with the security of your indulgence bank, people tend to be a bit more forgiving, understanding, and even helpful when things go off the rails.

Simply because, you put the time and effort into getting off to a good start.

You know well enough to not abuse it, but that support will carry you through good times and rough patches for you and your brand.

Through the course of this series I'll share some media planning, and buying experiences and strategies I hope you'll find advantageous to you and your business.

Stay tuned,

P.S. One of the most forward thinking moments arrived in 1964. Here's a hint, it was not The Beatles

Media Spike #2 – Do You Like My Tie?

Greetings.

So, how do I look?

Is my tie on straight?

Hair combed?

Freshly shaved?

Can you tell since you're only reading me? Probably not.

Do you care? Maybe, but I doubt it.

But perhaps you should because my manner of dress is an outward reflection of what's going on inside. Don't discount the value of packaging!

When I look good, I feel good. If I feel good, I believe I do better work, feeling the part. These are all connected.

When you surround yourself with quality, style and class, you tend to reflect that back to your viewers, readers, listeners, no matter how they receive your messages.

Even if my communication to you is non-visual, I will exude that aura of confidence in my voice, my writing, my every mannerism will be on display based on how I dressed.

You can be certain your audience is looking for any and all clues to gauge your level of quality, and the calibre of performance they can expect to see or hear or read from you.

We opened this series with the urging of making a good First Impression.

That will always stand you in good stead.

That does not, for a moment, give you license, to treat the 2nd impression and each one after that as inconsequential.

You are advertising **YOU**. The brand you are developing is you, my reader, and I want to make certain you are on your game, all the time, in every media, to every viewer, reader and listener.

The continuity of the brand from media to media is vital to sustaining the image, reputation, and viability now, and moving forward.

You should use multiple media to communicate your message. But that message should be consistent from media to media to ensconce trust and confidence.

Several clients through the years have developed some cracker-jack campaigns. Exceptionally Powerful. Insightful. Traffic Stoppers. Sales Generators.

Then they take that hard earned image and try to shoehorn it into an incompatible media, which diminishes its cache overnight.

It can take a lifetime to build a good reputation, and only seconds to destroy it when positioning is changed from its intent.

Here's a brief story, which may echo some familiarity for you:

Several years back, one computer printer client had a leg up on the competition due to a proprietary ink cartridge system.

The colour reproduction was crisper, cleaner, and the nuances between shades could be distinguished more readily than ever. Impressive stuff.

• This was an exciting opportunity to showcase this in the richness of high-end Consumer and Trade Magazines.

• Vibrant Backlit Outdoor media to demonstrate magnified detail.

• A foray into On-Line would have been a perfect launchpad.

While I pressed long and hard for these to be the media of choice, it was decided that daily Newspapers would be the deliverer of this new eye-popping colour explosion printer.

Believe me, no one has more affection and appreciation of the longevity of newsprint and the relationship it has with readers than yours truly.

However, the reproduction capabilities of colour on newsprint, while better now, left much to be desired at the time.

Several pricey ads were rendered unreadable on newsprint.

The older printing presses could not do justice to the look necessary to make this an enviable printer to purchase.

All the effort the creative team went to, to straighten their tie, and polish up the ad. And the production team combed their hair, making sure colour balances were their best.

All that combined effort could not undo the misstep of utilizing a media, which typically had better strengths elsewhere than colour reproduction. To suggest the end result was not flattering is being kind.

Sadly, that was a disheartening first impression for this new product launch.

On the plus side, it showed the client, more powerfully than anything I could say, it demonstrated to them firsthand the need for media which has the integrity of the look of the brand at its core each time.

Subsequent campaigns changed media mixes. Newsprint was still a vital part of the campaign, but was smartly used for the strength of text delivery and less for graphics at that time.

Does this mean don't use Newspapers? Hardly.

Despite erosion to the digital world, print media remain an important component to our communications for large and small clients alike. Here's a recent example. One client launched a Newspaper campaign with this decidedly edgy creative.

Brand: Clearnail™, Ad Agency: Orange Bazooka- Creative Director Rob Worling.

Strategic placement of this creative on Newspaper banner positions, which didn't break the bank, raised eyebrows and profile, and most importantly- made the phone ring for appointments.

Twenty years later, colour reproduction in Newspapers is much, much better.

But it's vital, I believe, that your media vehicles, whichever they may be, are well chosen and adaptable to the message.

You must maintain the integrity of the brand, allowing it to shine through no matter how your audience experiences it.

Tell me please, Do you like my tie?

Stay tuned,

P.S. The year 1964 brought The Beatles to America. Musically nothing rivals them before or since. But the forward thinking statement of that year-perhaps decade- came from Marshall McLuhan who famously coined the phrase ' The Medium Is The Message'.

Solidifying his reputation of being ahead of his time, he opined ***that not only is the content of the message you deliver important, the media you choose to deliver that message is as important as the content itself***. Smart guy this Mr. M.

P.P.S – One simple step could save you as much as 50% of your media spend. Want to know what it is?

Media Spike #3 – The Secret Sauce To A Long Relationship Is Caffeine!

Thanks for joining me again.

Do you like coffee?

I love my coffee. Every morning I get a medium black with one sugar.

As automatic as the sun rising, I get a coffee and it sets the tone for me for the rest of my day.

I have become so inextricably joined to it, that on those rare occasions when I've forgotten, my head starts pounding with caffeine withdrawal reminding me of my fix.

This coffee chain has promised me a quality product and delivered it to me each time. They understand an important business strategy, and that is the value of a long-term customer.

They have nurtured this along slowly and ensured I was a regular consumer and they could gradually offer me new and different products they added to their mix.

Does **your** advertising do that?

Are you consistently, persistently in front of your customers, and prospects on an ongoing basis?

Are you researching their wants and needs, or does it resemble a hunt and kill for one big sale, then move on in search of a brand new customer all over again?

I've often felt that advertising for most clients, maybe you feel this way too, should be more akin to an ongoing dating process.

Always trying to impress the girl with great service, a new look.

A variety of enticements, from chocolates and flowers, to dinners and shows, and always keeping it on that level.

She should hear a compliment from you everyday. How she looks. Pretty blouse. Flattering dress. Nice shoes. How she always captures your heart.

With consistent reassurance and affection, she will keep coming back, and coming back, and staying with you. She will have eyes for no other.

This is how I think your advertising, in media and all other communications, should be deployed.

Consistently. Persistently. Putting solutions in front of them, which genuinely resolve a problem or make their job easier.

In our last message, we asked you to stay tuned for a simple step that can save you lots of money for your ad budget. And we have it for you today.

But just before we reveal that, we want you to take notice of this,

Your advertising is more alike to dating than you perhaps realize.

It should be relationship building. It needs time to nurture and develop, and you want to treat this as an ongoing process and not just a final sale, but a customer for a lifetime of sales.

The hard part of course is keeping it fresh and relevant.
No woman, or client, wants to be courted the same way day after day after day after….

Rather, it should be as varied as your resources will allow, but as consistent as possible to ensure she knows it could only come from you.

At the moment, in no particular order, your courting efforts may get started with an introductory post card, soon after that, a quick, informative letter, perhaps an e-mail, then a phone call to put a voice to the source. Maybe it's time to interject a light promotion and suggest a lunch together.

Follow that up with another letter solving a problem and then a further postcard, and maybe host a seminar, or step it up to more powerful media including Newspaper, and On-line and Radio and Magazine and Television.

And while all these elements are in play, you keep consistent, persistent awareness of who you are, what you offer, in front of them.

Too many ad campaigns and dates I'm sure, go right for the jugular.

They try for the big sales on the first date, and not enough time building the relationship to ensure loyalty is ongoing.

Taking a cue from my own advice, I'll be back soon.

Stay tuned,

P.S. This is such a staggering ploy it eludes me why more large and small advertisers don't do it.

Want to save money on your advertising? I mean 'really save some money?'

Few other tactics work as well as ***buying early.*** When it's February, start booking your Radio or TV time for October.

Your rates will be as much as 50%* cheaper than only booking your schedule two or three weeks ahead of time. Supply and demand. (* varies by station and market)

Media Spike #4 – When Cooler Heads Prevail

Glad you stopped by.

Recently one client asked me to comment on the potential choice of Radio stations in two different markets.

That's fine. It's part of what I do and I was glad to respond.

It poses a bit of a quagmire potential because so many factors influence the choice of station(s) for any campaign.

Thus I resisted the temptation to jump in without taking a breath and firing any answer off the top of my head.

Partly because I had the luxury of this coming via e-mail, it gave me time to consider and digest this question before responding.

There's nothing wrong with crafting a well thought out answer.

In today's speed at all costs mentality, the cost is very often rushed and incorrect or based on flimsy information. Which begets having to do it over again to get it right.

Therefore I properly researched the two markets in question. Identified the 21 and 8 Radio stations per market respectively.

Secured a 3rd party industry ranking of how each station was performing based on most recent survey details.

My response to her:

• Commented on the stations she had considered in each market.
• Then provided a more thoroughly researched, articulate, defendable summary
• This allowed me the confidence to acknowledge her choices, but the empirical backing to state why I believed other stations would be better candidates.

Will any new business come of it? Maybe. But for now that is secondary.

I'm continuing to nurture trust with this client. I am building my credibility with her. She needs to know I won't blindly endorse one opportunity without conducting due diligence on it.

Maybe this could be a component of your long-term strategy as well.

Do we want to make the sale? Of course! But we want to ensure we make more than just one sale. You and I each need to educate our clients and prospects about whatever it is they've asked about. Developing this positioning as the 'Go To Guy' (or girl) is what will separate you from the other contenders and pretenders.

Your clients are coming to you for solutions. Establish yourself as the one who can provide them and you'll never lack for customers.

Stay tuned,

P.S. Is it more work to cultivate business this way?

That depends on what you want to accomplish.

It's more work to lay the foundation of a long-term relationship and continue to foster growth with professional, smart, informative, helpful solutions so that you are continually enhancing the long-term value of this client.

Or, you can develop a new pitch every week for a series of one-time potential successes, but you need to keep going further and further a field to attract new candidates for your once and done approach. Your choice.

Media Spike #5 - The Power of Advance Notice

Welcome back.

Thanks for taking my call.
We just heard that you landed this account and think our magazine would be a
great place for you to advertise, and I can come by in twenty minutes to pick up
your order and can you have a $7,500 deposit cheque ready, and we'll need new
creative by the end of the week.

The frightening part is, this scenario, with minor industry variations, is re-enacted
by thousands of sales professionals everyday.

Anxious to make that one-time kill now that they've found your phone number, it
somehow gives them license to believe they can bully and harangue you until you
place the order.

Perhaps they are driven to achieve a specific sales quota by the end of the
week/month/quarter and it has to be done NOW, NOW, NOW!

I have worked with too many hardworking, talented sales professionals who are
genuinely in it for the long term, to float anything disparaging out there. I enjoy
business relationships of a couple of decades with many of them, despite the
changes in employers for each of us.

It is this commitment to the long-term, which has made them prized allies for me.
But I fear they are in the minority, as the immediate sale always seems to be the
name of the game.

Perhaps if the initial paragraph is too representative of your sales approach, you
might consider a longer view of the process - it is a process after all.

One of my favourite ads, maybe one of yours too, depicts the power of advance
education about your product or service. More recently, there are strategies of
relationship building. Providing free advice upfront in exchange for contact info.

Getting your name, product, service in front of your desired target group is
always the name of the game. Build that relationship and recognition long before
you walk into their doors.

Among the best at doing this for many years is Magazines. Magazines have been
playing the ice-breaker to many business relationships for decades. They are your
emissary, your envoy or ambassador announcing who you are and what you offer
before you make a personal appearance.

Witness this Timeless Classic ad by McGraw Hill Magazines™*

A rather dour businessman is seated in his office chair, staring back at you.

The copy bullets beside him read

I don't know who you are
I don't know your company.
I don't know what your company stands for.
I don't know your company's customers.
I don't know your company's record.
I don't know your company's reputation.
Now – what was it you wanted to sell me?

* You can find a copy of this ad in our Magazines article by clicking here:
http://firstimpressionsmedia.ca/media-library-and-articles--free-.html

Who wants to buy from you if they've never heard of you?

Regardless of your product or service, you can never overeducate a client or customer.

Don't hesitate to give them information that helps them, by providing a solution, which also positions you as an expert resource.

The relationship you build with your ads is equally vital. Regardless of which media combinations you choose (yes you should always use more than one form- but that's another topic) the conversation in your ads should be the solution they need to the challenge already going on in their own heads.

When this education is in place, the initial paragraph scenario should sound more like:

Thanks for taking my call. Congratulations on winning that new account. How Can I Help?

Stay tuned,

P.S. There is always more synergy, impact, reach and memorability when you add a secondary media instead of just buying more of the first.

Media Spike #6 – Spend Smarter, Not Just More!

Hi, hope you're having a great day.

Recently one client asked about a small on-line campaign we were developing for them. I was, naturally very pleased they liked our media recommendation, but a bit disconcerted at the question.

Are the 50,000 impressions on site XYZ going to be enough over 4 weeks? Should we buy more just in case?

You can never give a media buyer-that's me- too much money. However, she was asking as though just the incremental weight was all that would be required to guarantee a winner.

There are just too many variables that influence responses - in all media.

Certainly having adequate presence is among them.
Choosing the right site or sites contributes as well.
The nature of the creative is a key element.
> Is it engaging?
> Will it pull you in enough to stimulate a 'click' to get to your site?
> Is there any other media support to bolster awareness?
> How much equity is there, if any, in the brand being advertised?

To suggest, or hope it can all be fixed, or made better by throwing more at it is not the ideal strategy in our estimation.

We'd love to see this campaign do extremely well.

We want that for every campaign.

But the only way to know - to really know if this on-line campaign is working is to test it. Measure it. See what level of response it generates, rather than increasing the spend at the outset.

Before opening up the wallet even further, we countered with this proposal.

> Keep the proposed weight the same of 50,000 impressions.
> Shorten the flight.
> Make it two weeks instead of four weeks.
> The budget will not change.
> You'll increase the weight per week.
> You'll have two weeks – which is a lifetime on-line, for some testing.

Then after two weeks, when all 50,000 Impressions have been deployed through different creative sizes on different positions on the site, you'll have a benchmark of what's working, or not, and can adjust accordingly.

My client was taken aback.

You're the first person to suggest something other than just spend more money.

That's why we believe it's **Your Advertising. Well Planned. Well Spent.**

Stay tuned,

P.S. You will see me make multiple references to the merits of Testing throughout this series. The idea is not new. Industry giant, Mr. John Caples was deemed the father of Testing to see what works, and what doesn't in your ads. (We will learn more of Mr. John Caples talents later in this series)

A more prominent voice on this matter today is Mr. Chris Cardell in the United Kingdom. He distills it simply to say that Marketing is Testing.

You can learn a great deal more from Mr. Cardell by clicking here:
http://www.cardellmedia.com/marketing-testing.html

P.P.S. Your Marketing is your lifeline. Cut this budget and you slice your jugular. Always be in front of your audience. And do it smartly and with integrity. You will be remembered by the lowest denominator you select. Choose wisely.

Media Spike #7 – STOP it Right Now !!

Welcome along.

Is your advertising working as hard as you are?

Genuinely? Is it? Is it stimulating awareness?

Provoking trial by purchase?

Inciting repeat purchases by more and more customers?

If it is, break out the champagne and celebrate. That's fabulous.

If it's not doing any of those things- then **STOP.**

Right now. STOP your campaign dead in its tracks.

The whole intent of your advertising is to generate sales.
Sometimes that's an immediate lift in response as measured at the cash register.

Sometimes it's a measurable call to action to visit a website and get a coupon, a free report, or to place a phone call for more information.

Sadly most advertising fails to leave a mark.
Worse, it fails to make a sale. Even enough sales to justify the cost of the ad process, from concept to placement.

So if you can look at your ads right now, and they're not working- then stop them, NOW!!

Some years back I had a very prominent specialized financial lender a client who used business Newspapers, and a few Magazines very smartly.

His audience was well targeted. His ads were well written. An engaging testimonial style, with an inviting headline for each of them.

Beneath their logo they placed a 1-800 Number for anyone to call in.

They did this for two years and enjoyed great response by all accounts.

One fateful year, they asked about the relevance of the 1-800 Number.

I suggested customizing it a bit more by adding a specific 'Extension' number in the ad. Or to ask for a certain person whose name appeared in the ad.

This way it could be accurately measured and tracked which ads were working, and which inquiries were coming from which papers in each market.

This was dismissed as being unnecessary as they 'had a pretty good idea' where the replies were coming from even though they couldn't measure it.

I don't know about you dear reader, but when I'm spending $100,000 on a campaign, **I WANT TO KNOW** where my replies are coming from, not just a pretty good idea!

It is sometimes heartbreaking the apathy which pervades too many companies who have such disdain for their own marketing. I had a very recent exchange with a former colleague who posed a similar 'Tracking' request to our largest client of the day.

The client's response was so sad: *Just spend the money. Head office gives us the money to spend, so spend it.*

My creative teams and media colleagues and I are busting ourselves to deliver the best product our services can render and to find someone who has nowhere near the same passion just crushes spirit. And many of these same companies are wondering, Gee why are sales down this quarter? Go figure.

That media budget is the most precious marketing resource you have. I will never, ever treat it as inconsequential. To make it work as hard as possible,

I WANT TO KNOW
Which ads are working?.
How are they working?.
Are we getting a better response from ad A or B or C ?.
This is the underpinning to all future successes.
TEST your ads. Track what's working or not.

It strikes me that too many advertisers are worried about the cosmetics of the ad and less about the return it can deliver. The role of your advertising is to make sales.

You don't have to take my word for it.

There is a century old benchmark of what advertising is,....but that's for another day.

For today, concentrate on **Stopping** your advertising that's ineffective, dull, boring, and not driving any business. That first step to Stop will be a pivotal moment for you and your future success.

You've worked hard to get this far. Don't let your advertising let you down.

Stay tuned,

P.S.   Recently someone posed the question of why I advocate TESTING. Heck let's just put all our media muscle behind the campaign and run with it. Hmmm?

Trouble is, without knowing if it's working, you can run the campaign off an expensive cliff and suffer a very pricey fail.

Here's a favourite analogy for you: *You don't need to eat a whole bowl of soup to discover if it's too salty. One or two spoonfuls should tell you.* Treat your campaign the same way.

Media Spike #8 – What's Your Wavelength?

Thanks for taking the time to join me.

Not too long ago I heard a familiar statement from one client who said they'd like to start advertising again.

I replied with customary – WONDERFUL!! enthusiasm and began asking a few questions.

Well that's exciting Peter, have you thought about which media you'd like to use? Without missing a beat, Peter said, *'Absolutely, we're going to use Radio!'*

An excellent choice I countered, how are you going to use it?
This prompted the first of a series of quizzical looks?

What do you mean, how? We're going to be on Radio.

Yes, and that's exciting but HOW do you intend to use it?

A blank stare met this second question.

Okay Peter, here's what I mean.

Radio is deemed both the physical unit, which delivers the sound via airwaves, as well as the media which communicates with no visual experience. Because each of us experiences Radio through the listening to our own tastes, time, and location, Radio has become a very personal experience.

Unlike Television, where viewers are program loyal, Radio listeners are station loyal and tend to keep it fixed on one dial position for the majority of their tuning day.

What we want to do in our Radio advertising is find the best station or stations that our target group is listening to. Put our message in their ears on an ongoing basis, in a format that is appealing and relevant to them.

Peter was non-plussed so far. *But Dennis you told me that Radio reaches over 90% of Adult listeners every week. What difference would it make, as long as we're on 'Radio'?*

Peter does raise a valid point. Nearly every forum of advertising is good and it will help get your name and message out there.

But the important part of putting that sparkling message out there is making sure it reaches the people who count, and you're not just counting the people you reach. The way you reach them is the How, I was asking about.

Let's just take our home base to start with, Peter.

We are in a prominent city in Canada.

We have, in our city alone, twenty-one (21) Radio stations at this writing.

Each of them with a different mix of music, personalities, information, sports, talk, weather, language, and everyone of them looking for your advertising dollars.

In each of those stations, the audience composition will vary depending on gender, age, education, musical tastes, affection for the Radio personalities at each daypart, and the location (home/drive/office/patio/other) of the listener.

Peter was starting to shift his weight, that kind of glazed over look was forming. *Wait a minute. Are you saying that all of this happens on each station!?!*

Yes Peter. That's it exactly. In addition, when Radio airtime is sold, it can typically be sold as a 60 second commercial, or 30 second commercial and there are options for using a 15 second spot now as well.

These are often sold in timeblocks or 'daypart' segments best known as

- Breakfast: 5.30am – 10.00am
- Day: 10.00am – 3.00pm
- Drive: 3.00pm – 8.00pm
- Evening: 8.00pm-1.00am

There are sometimes minor variations from market to market and station to station, but in the majority, these are the segments you are purchasing.

You might already know, Peter, these are typically sold as a Reach Plan meaning you purchase an equal number of spots in each of the dayparts. For example, it can be a 16, 20, 24, 28, 32 spot weekly reach plan. Meaning that each of our 4 dayparts would air 4 , 5, 6, 7, or 8 spots per week.

This gives you a balanced rotation of commercials to stay with your listeners all day and enhance recall all week.

It also means that deeper pocketed advertisers don't swoop all the 'Breakfast' period spots and leave the rest of the day to other advertisers.

So, Peter asked, if I only wanted say 20 Breakfast spots per week, I couldn't do it?

Well, depending on the stations' available inventory, you might be able to, but it commands such a high rate premium to isolate just one daypart that it's often not advantageous to do this.

You pay a very high price to reach the same audience, and only those listeners, multiple times. It's a smarter strategy to extend the reach using multiple dayparts, AND if budget allows, to use multiple Radio stations.

Does this mean I have to buy reach plans?

Not at all. There are multiple opportunities for you to buy just a specific daypart, but higher premiums may deter you.

Some stations will allow you to go a bit heavier on some dayparts where it's more relevant for you.

Ie: Move a spot or two from each of Day and Evening into Drive daypart if you offer say 'Take Out Food' and want to reach the crowd going home after work.

One strategy we've used to great effect, and it's easy to do, is to buy a sponsorship package.

What does that mean, posed Peter?

It means Peter, it's time to exhale for today and continue this discussion tomorrow. See you then.

Stay tuned,

Media Spike #9 – Close Your Eyes and Listen

Greetings once again.

So glad you could join us for a few minutes.

You might remember yesterday, we were having a great discussion with Peter.

He was asking what it meant to purchase a Radio sponsorship.

What it means, Peter, is you are making a purchase to be specifically aligned to a particular report so that listeners get to know you as the one always associated with that feature.

To make it worthwhile for both the advertiser and the station, these are usually 13 week features, although shorter flights are possible.

Ideally you want a feature that ties into your product or service if available:

> Ie: Today's Ski Report is brought to you by Razor's Edge Ski Wax*

> This Traffic Report is brought to you by See Your Way Clear Windshield Wipers*

> This Daily Business Report is brought to you by Retirement Mutual Funds*

(* all fictitious names. Any similarity to actual products is purely coincidental)

It doesn't have to be an exact match, but it makes a great affiliation and name recall if the ad and the report are closely aligned.

So, Peter asked, is this all I need? Just one sponsorship and don't do anything else?

Interesting question. If funds are limited, a sponsorship is an excellent way to target a very specific audience- your audience- and make sure you maximize your exposure to them. Even if you have more than enough funds, a sponsorship is an excellent way to be in front of your audience on a regular basis.

If I have the opportunity, certainly I'd add more Radio time and more media to my buy. But this can be an excellent starting point and anchor for any campaign.

Just know that within Radio and all media, there are multiple layers of choices for where and how to invest those ad dollars.

Until we revisit this, you can also take a peek at our Radiowaves PDF found here:

http://firstimpressionsmedia.ca/media-library-and-articles--free-.html

This will offer you some additional ammunition as you're planning.

Stay tuned,

P.S: The Power of Theatre Of The Mind Radio: Some readers may remember 'The Lone Ranger', a very popular TV series, which ran in the late 1940's and early 1950's. It was also recently a feature film, which had limited success.

But before movies and TV, The Lone Ranger was an immensely popular Radio series, which started in 1933, and aired over 2,900 Radio episodes.

And no-one could see him, but everyone knew exactly what he looked like. The Power of Radio is as visual as your imagination.

Media Spike #10 – START The Presses!

Hope it's a great day. Thanks for coming along.

Believe me, I didn't forget you.

We've only known each other a little while now, but I wouldn't forget you. In a recent message, we advised there is a century old benchmark for advertising.

More than 100 years later, this definition is masterful in its brevity and has never been improved upon.

Quite simply: **Advertising is Salesmanship in Print.**

That line is attributed to John E. Kennedy in 1904. He joined Albert Lasker's, Lord & Thomas advertising agency in Chicago and went on to enjoy some grand success as a copywriter.

Not surprising that it took a copywriter to distill it to its very essence.

It seems the faster and faster communication has evolved to be, the less and less we communicate. You have to learn to like living by initials apparently, as no-one has time for full words these days.

Yes I get we're all in a hurry- where we are all rushing to I'm not sure, but we are racing there at blinding speed.

Only to arrive and then jump on the next hover-board or jet pack and be whisked to another dimension where we have an even bigger in-tray to wade through.

In the face of all this, isn't it refreshing to read?

Multiple lines. Full sentences, which articulate a thought or a sports story or the news from across the country. A century ago, the speed of life was as fast as a railway train, and Newspapers were a learned man's bible.

There is a perception running rampant that Newspapers are on the endangered species. A fear which, if left unchecked, will certainly hasten its demise.

However, in spite of increased competition from broadcast media, and the omnipresent world of online, Newspapers continue to enjoy a loyal readership and trustworthiness with the reader.

At this writing, there are 122 daily Newspapers published in Canada. Fully 77% of them paid circulation, the balance are free distribution. Our appetite for the written word is insatiable.

Although many papers have a sister version via on-line, or they mirror their print edition with an electronic one on their website, the printed edition continues to be the most popular way to enjoy the Newspaper.

Today, more than a century later, the train can't match the speed of e-mail, nor be as trend-setting as a carbon-fibre bicycle, or the next self-propelled invention, but even if your train ride is only a commute to the office, it's a great place to read the Newspaper isn't it?

So what did Mr. Kennedy teach us in this iconic phrase of 100+ years ago?

Quite simply, I believe, that our salesmanship, in any and all media, is how we weave 26 letters to create compelling stories to touch one another's hearts. The words we use to persuade another to take a particular course of action, including purchasing our product, are at the core of every message.

Do I want you to use different media combinations?

Absolutely. But the media is only the carrier of your message.

Your message has to be leading the charge.
Your media mix will increase your chances of your message being seen. How you weave the alphabet will be the trigger for action.

Stay tuned,

P.S. Closing with a nostalgic sales pitch: Read All About It!!

Welcome To Checkpoint Number One

A summary of our first 10 Media Spikes together.

#1: Make sure in EVERY ad, you always give yourself the chance to look your very best. It may be the ONLY time a prospect sees you. Look your best, always.

#2: Remember to use each media at your disposal for their respective strength. You want every one of your ads in each media to deliver Stopping Power.

#3: Be consistently, persistently in front of your clients with your message. You earn their trust and become a valuable ally and not an annoying peddler.

#4: Take the time to deliver your answers CORRECTLY. In this pell-mell pace of response, we note Speed begets errors, errors beget re-do, re-do compromises confidence.

#5: Be the MC for yourself and your service. Make yourself known and valuable before even attempting a sale.

#6: Demonstrate some creative solutions to challenges as they arise.
Don't just throw more client money at the issue without thinking through
a smarter solution.

#7: If your ads aren't working, **STOP** right now. Fix them. Test them small. When you have small successes, then, and only then go bigger.

#8: Radio: Among the best salespersons ever because all the activity happens in your imagination. You are creating the visual clues in your own mind. AND, - to the best of your budget, we encourage you to use multiple stations and multiple dayparts for maximum impact.

#9: Radio: Don't dismiss the value of a Sponsorship. It can very quickly give you a recognizable identity.

#10: Advertising continues to be Salesmanship in Print. The Power of the alphabet is unmatched.

It remains my privilege to be welcomed into your day. Thank you. The Media Spikes will resume their standard delivery pattern. If at any time you have any media questions, I look forward to hearing from you.

Stay tuned,

Media Spike #11 – What's Your Favourite Number?

Welcome Back.

Hope you're having a great day today.

Are you one in a million?
Perhaps one in 100,000?
Maybe sneaking in there at one in 3,000?

The hardest part of making yourself memorable is finding a way to **STAND OUT.**

In a sea of daily messages, it has been estimated we are exposed to upwards of 3,000 advertising and marketing messages each day.

That will be enormously inflated or woefully inadequate, depending on whom you consult.

Even erring very conservatively to say we are exposed to only 10% of that, that's still 300 messages daily.

Starting with the packaging from your soap and toothpaste providers each morning, to your coffee, juice, cereal sources, plus the pitches from Radio and TV in the morning as well as e-mail and spam messages.

Let's not forget the images you see on your way to work, on the train or bus, on other vehicles, on fixed signage outside, on ads in the Newspaper your busmate is reading, ...and when you go through your entire day- in and out of the office, to school, the health club, and the grocery store.

Of course there's the prospect of further ads at the movie theatre, the golf course, the restaurant, the gas station, the convenience store, the parking garage, there is an endless barrage of sales messages you absorb every day.

Do you remember any of them?

Could you recollect five of them for me now?

Go ahead- take a minute. It's just between us. Let me see....did you see an ad for

Fresh bagels?
Shoe repair?
Fresh breath?
Fast food?
Financial service?

Give yourself a point for each category you remember. Now double the points if you can remember even three of the brand names you saw.

We are a forgetful group.

Phone number of your first employer when you had a part-time job in high school. No sweat: 555-735-7282.
Dennis – what'd you have for lunch today?...Ummmm?

This is what advertisers thrive on. We need to have constant repetition of the message until it becomes part of our subconscious.

So how often is enough?

The answer to that alone could make one very wealthy. A new brand needs a lot more exposure to get started and build up some profile and equity for the long term.

More established brands have already paid their dues. While they are constantly refining themselves, to stay relevant and fresh, today they enjoy the residual of decades of advertising history, which make them household names across the planet.

It's been expressed in various circles that a 3 to 5 times frequency during a campaign is a good barometer to work towards as far as establishing some breakthrough and recognition.

Conversely it's been noted it can take 6 to 8 points of contact- ads, e-mail, phone call, newsletter, etc. before people respond to you.

Perhaps the optimal is to keep marketing all the time.

Maybe, not always at the same intensity, unless your wallet can handle this.

But continually have some presence out there. You will grow tired of your messaging before your audience does. If they see you in multiple places, over a longer period of time, you will earn their trust and confidence.

As that exposure delivers more awareness and sales, you'll be better able to keep up the marketing efforts. As we've expressed to date, we are trying to build long-term customer relationships.

If we make an initial sale, that's great. But we are striving to compete head-on with potentially multiple thousands of other messages every day.

To paraphrase legendary marketer Roy Williams: Despite your best efforts, you can't predict the moment any client will purchase any product or service you provide. But you must provide an ongoing stream of service samples and education so that when your client needs your product or service, you're the one they think of.

In order to make yourself stand out, **BE OUTSTANDING.**

Stay tuned,

P.S. One of the overlooked benefits of long-term exposure is how it seamlessly becomes part of the fabric and pattern of our daily lives.

When I was a younger- and thinner man- one prominent insurance company used two forms of advertising that I knew of. I heard them on the Radio as a regular feature sponsor, and they used exterior rear bus cards. That's IT.

But they were ALWAYS there. For more years than I care to remember, however that consistency made them memorable for me more than 4 decades later.

Media Spike #12 – Hard Hitting Vocabulary!

Hello and thanks for coming.

Has this ever happened to you? It occurred to me very recently and I wondered if I was the only one to experience this.

Someone said a new phrase. It hit me **like a thunderclap.**

When I'm not writing to you, I'm often attending meetings at a prominent, international, speaking organization. These meetings help improve your Public Speaking skills and they foster leadership skills.

One of our members was commenting on another members' speech that evening. Her accolades and critiques were well delivered and I was concurring with her observations.

She then said, *I think you might find it helpful to consider doing XYZ as it will help you* **'Punctuate Your Point'.**

That line stopped me cold. ***Punctuate Your Point.***

Your advertising needs to do exactly that. Quickly. Creatively. Efficiently. Tell the reader what they get by using your product or service.

Make your message POP off the page. Fill eardrums. Enlarge eyeballs.
Deliver it with panache and IMPACT.

Whichever media you use, don't give away your time at bat. In the words of former clergyman turned writer Basil King, *Be Bold, And Mighty Forces Will Come To Your Aid.*

THAT'S *Punctuating Your Point.*

Stay tuned,

P.S. Why should you use Radio with Newspaper ads? What's the point of a poster campaign with exterior bus cards and ½ page magazine ads? Why don't we just use the Internet for everything?

And the answer is………coming soon to this same space.

Media Spike #13 – How Can I Help You?

Oh good, you're here. Nice to have you join me again.

It started out as an ordinary, unassuming day, but fates intervened and suddenly I was hurtled into a frenetic pace of action. The best-laid plans went out the window in a heartbeat. Files scoured. Records unearthed. Favours called in. Phone lines on fire. E-mails seemed too slow to help me through this whirlwind which now consumed me. Breathing became shallow and rapid. My pulse hadn't raced like this since a 3 foot putt. If a Commissioner's Hotline had been available, this would have been the time to call in legendary assistance.

Alone. The task loomed large in front of me. No fancy words or tap-dancing would extricate me from this moment of truth.

Collecting myself, ...drawing breath,....I fixed my gaze......and with controlled poise, I spoke those immortal words that changed my career forever......

Hello. How Can I Help You Today?

Does your advertising deliver a story? A Reason Why the product or service should be used or purchased?

Your advertising is to demonstrate through words and pictures that you have **THE** solution to whatever the challenge is of that day for the customer right in front of you.

Do they need a new writer? Maybe a Graphic Designer to freshen up their look? A sharp media buyer to save money, and help them look good?

You might recollect our opening line in this series that your advertising is **Your** platform. Your chance to shine, but you must not confuse this with being about you. It's about your customer.

That self absorbed individual who is only looking out for their own wants and needs and looking for you to take away pain or give them pleasure.

The media you choose, that's your platform.

The message, your sales pitch, is dependent on you creating the right words, delivered with the right media.

The audience? Your buyers. They are waiting to be sold to. And they will LOVE to be sold to, as long as you're genuinely helping them with a solution to their challenge of the day.

Hello again dear reader. How Can I Help You Today?

Stay tuned,

P.S. Ever use a sand wedge from 245 yards? How about a putter from the sand trap? No?...Funny because that's what many advertisers do with their campaigns. Stick around, we'll show you how to avoid these hiccups.

Media Spike #14 – There Is NO Failure When You Test. Only Results.

Greetings and let me ask you, How much is too much?

When do you know if you're spreading yourself too thin?

Powerful questions. All the more reason that you need to keep testing.

Testing your media. Testing your creative.
Always measuring what works and what can get relegated to the sidelines.

Testing can reveal concerns on a small scale before they become huge, costly blunders.

No-one, big or small wants to discover they've blown the annual campaign budget on a strategy and selection that didn't work.

It can take a long time to recover from that kind of scar.

More than a few clients have disdained the value of Testing. Dismissing it as inconsequential. Their gut is usually a good barometer of what works.

In fairness, sometimes they're right. They play a hunch and it pays off. But I'd like you to rely on something more reliable and repeatable than a 'feeling' for the right strategy.

Would more sales convince you? What if you could double your sales? (No?) How about triple them? (Still not enough for you?)

How about **19 ½ TIMES** More sales? Would that be enough to convince you there is merit in constant testing?

Legendary copywriter John Caples was forever Testing what worked and continually refined it until he hit that repeatable Grand Slam home run with his ad. His most memorable experience is distilled on our article entitled Now's Your Chance. You'll find it by clicking the link below.

John Caples on Now's Your Chance

What Mr. Caples revealed was that in Testing there is no failure. **There is NO Failure…there is only Results.**

When you have the results from your testing, then you can better determine How Much is Enough. And how to not spread yourself too thin.

Two good rules of thumb, especially if you're starting out are as follows:

1. Work hard to secure as much Free, Complimentary, No Charge exposure as you can to build up your name and product or service. Write articles. Provide Free tips. Do speaking engagements if your industry calls for it (maybe especially if they don't). Get as much mileage on a shoestring as possible.

2. If funds are kinda tight, probably best to stick to one media and watch it very closely to see how it performs. If you generate enough sales to cover the ad, plus some left over, then keep reinvesting till you generate enough sales and revenue to consider adding another media to your mix. Remember you're testing all along.

Don't just take your sales rep's word for it. Test each Newspaper ad you run. Monitor closely how great a response your Radio ads deliver. Did the On-Line ads drive enough traffic to your site? Did it deliver a click? Did it spark a sale?

It's only by testing will you truly appreciate how much you need and what works on a small scale before rolling it out on a bigger platform.

It's much better to fail small in order to learn to win big, than to reverse those.

Stay tuned,

P.S. In case you were wondering, John Caples wrote the legendary ad: **They Laughed When I Sat Down At The Piano**, in 1926. It remains a classic by which thousands of successors are measured.

You'll find a copy with full size readable copy by clicking here or by visiting this link:

http://swiped.co/file/they-laughed-when -i-sat-down-at-the-piano-by-john-caples/

Media Spike #15 – Here, There, and Everywhere? Why Not!!

Come on in, come on in, we're just about to start. Come on in.

If you've been paying attention, and at a dozen + message into this series I'm sure you have, you'll note at the end of Media Spike #11 we asked in our P.S.

• Why should you use Radio and couple it with Newspaper ads?
• What's the point of a colourful poster campaign with exterior bus cards and supporting that with four colour ½ page, horizontal magazine ads?
• Why don't we just use the Internet for everything?

Despite yours and mine best intentions, people, our customers, have this annoying habit of using more than one media to get their information.

Sometimes it's a Radio news station with On-Line broadcasting.
Or sometimes they read a Newspaper on their way to work, two days a week, but the other three days they carpool and don't see your ad.
Once in a while they might tune to a TV program, but flip to the sports highlights elsewhere just as your commercial airs.

These fickle prospects compel us to use all means at our disposal, and in our budget to get in front of them on a regular basis until they take notice of us.

> Certainly some will be drawn in by your Newspaper ad, if the day is right and your ad hits them on the same day they're reading.

> Radio is a wonderful way to get between the ears. But maybe they have a no-Radio policy at work and they'll miss your ads all day.

> On-line can be an amazing place of engagement, but you'll be competing as a needle in the world's largest haystack with an estimated 50 Million Plus active websites out there.

> You selected just the perfect magazine mix and they love to read, but this month, the kids are sick, the car needs repairs and their work is crazy so you're unopened in an in tray!

The best way to combat this, once you've done your testing, is to implement proven multiple media to improve your chances of them seeing/hearing one or more messages to respond to.

Most of us, being capricious by nature, are susceptible to sudden and unaccountable changes of mood or behavior. As such, that which is riveting today, is invisible tomorrow.

By having multiple touchpoints of recognition in the marketplace, you increase your chances to be noticed and acted on.

In fairness, some clients have done exceedingly well relying on only one or two media through their history. But they've only reached that level of success by constantly changing and refining it until they can place it on autopilot.

Give yourself every chance for success by letting your prospects know you're here to help.

Stay tuned,

P.S. Remember, in the majority, you are not the target group for your own product. Get out of your shoes and into your customers'.

Media Spike #16 – Everything Old Is New Again.

Greetings once again, thanks for joining us for a few minutes today.

Are you a fan of Television?

Do you like just flipping the channels endlessly, or are there specific programs you'll make time for?

I ask because it seems Television has taken an unfair beating in recent decades.

Do you remember the enormously successful Back To the Future™ movie trilogy with actors Michael J. Fox and Christopher Lloyd? There's one scene where time traveling Marty McFly (Fox) finds himself seated at the dinner table with younger versions of his grandparents.

They're excited to see Jackie Gleason on the black & white TV. To Marty it was a classic 'rerun', to the rest it was brand new. The year was 1955 and television was just finding its mark.

It was a BIG DEAL to have a television back then and the technology was in its infancy by today's standards. But it set the stage for programming to evolve to bring us what we have on our screens today.

That may be better or worse, that's your discretion and choice and I'm not moralizing here. But, what I have noticed is the shorter and shorter attention spans we seem to have as viewers.

Programming now has to be lightning quick it seems to hold our interest.
Now you can have TV on your laptop. You can stream programming on other handheld devices. The technology is truly impressive. Frightening too, it seems, but impressive nonetheless.

So as an advertiser, what do you do?
Television is getting more and more splintered and fragmented.
Each new season unveils shows that make the first cut in the Fall, but fail to maintain our interest in the New Year.

Well-intended replacements are trotted out. More marketing muscle behind them. Some flourish. Some wither and don't even make it to 'Whatever Happened To' type of programming.

Despite this constant reinvention, Television lives. That is perhaps what keeps it fresh and relevant. It **IS** constantly being refreshed. New faces, styles, looks, program mixes. More sports. More skin. More drama. Less sitcom.

More reality…..and the tide will turn again where all of those mores are less, and less made more.

All in the interests of keeping you attracted to it. It is perhaps the ultimate wardrobe where if you don't like what you're wearing today, there's ALWAYS something new on the next hanger the next day.

Part of the trade here is that it continues to be among the most expensive options for marketing your products and services.   The nature of my work has allowed me to invest in a litany of Television programs for many clients- large and small- through the years.

Despite relatively deep pockets for one client, I was startled to find one program, offered at a Prime evening time slot was also a prime cost. One, just one, thirty-second spot on this program was a whopping $77,500. That's ONE (1) spot. At a time when other high-ended programming was commanding $25-$30K, this one leapt off the page.

It was tremendously efficient as it delivered a huge and targeted audience, but that level of investment is a full annual budget for many clients.

Television, just like all the other media players, is a powerful communication tool when used smartly. Locally, regionally, nationally, or internationally, Television commands attention.

In a preamble to a more detailed Golf analogy to follow in this series, Television continues to be the Driver in your Golf bag. You might not need it to play every hole, but people pay attention when you can lace your drive long and straight down the fairway.

Stay tuned,

P.S. In Media Spike #2 of this series, we mentioned Marshall McLuhan, a prominent Canadian professor and ultimately communications icon. His thinking still resonates today. I found this clip of his work and thought you might enjoy.

The Medium Is The Message

http://individual.utoronto.ca/markfederman/article_mediumisthemessage.htm

Media Spike # 17 – Alone Without Isolation

Welcome back. Hope you've had a great day.

As I write this, I can't help but be reminded of the seemingly endless variety of media, which are available at our fingertips today.

Equally how impressive it is we can use this electronic media *(remember Dear Book Readers, this began life as an e-mail series)* to communicate about the strengths, limitations and nuances of all the other media you encounter each day.

My office overlooks a deep pastoral-like setting of evergreens, cedars and a few colourful maple trees.

In the summer their shade is a welcome respite on a hot day. In fall, their colours blaze with fiery intensity few painters could capture. As the snow descends, they transform this setting into a picture perfect Christmas card scene.

Amidst this daily serenity,
- I am connected to the globe by the Internet.
- A Radio or CD often keeps me company in the background.
- My cellphone is at my side for immediate communications by voice or text.
- My landline is always at the ready.
- My in-tray is replete with current Magazines for multiple industries.
- When the day is done (or during the World Series) even a few moments of Television can find their way into my office.

It's not long ago each of these were dreams by pioneers. Now they have become so entrenched in our daily lives, we can't survive without needing to feel connected somewhere.

Truly I'm thrilled you've joined me for each Media Spike. You devote a few precious minutes to me and it's a privilege. Thank you.

How much more precious is the rest of your day? What other media are fighting for your attention all day?

Stand by, because in our next Spike, we're going to walk through the daily media assault on your senses.

Stay tuned,

P.S. Have a Great Day!

Media Spike #18 – A Minefield of Messages

Greetings and salutations.

With appropriate apologies to Mr.'s Paul McCartney and John Lennon, I will borrow from a Sgt. Pepper's Lonely Hearts Club Band album (©-Copyright 1967 The Beatles) track with an abridged title of 'A Day In The Life...of your Customer'.

You want to stand out. Make an IMPACT. Be memorable. Okay - here's a snippet of your daily competition, where you are trying to get noticed in this, message at every turn, lifestyle.

Our hero, Andy (insert heroine if you're so inclined) wakes up to the Radio, and an alarm, or song or ad catapults him from the bed to the floor to start the day.

Perhaps he flicks on the TV in the bedroom while getting ready for work. Maybe several ads appear during the weather for the day and the sports highlights. But there's a daily reminder of Branding on his toothpaste tube, on his soap and shampoo too.

If time permits, Andy has a moment for a quick check of his e-mail before leaving the house for work.

If Andy's a public transit guy, he picks up a Newspaper or magazine to read on his way to work. He will doubtless be exposed to ads on the outside and inside of buses and or subway/train halls/walls/corridors.

Chances are good he'll see some TV monitors in the subways and passing through food courts.

There may also be an ad on Andy's ticket or bus transfer, not to mention all the signage at every convenience store he passes along the way to the trains.

If Andy's driving today, he will see all the ads on buses, Outdoor ads, mobile ads on trucks passing by while he's listening to the car Radio.

Maybe, Andy, you've got headphones on to listen to the Radio station streamed from the lap-top computer while you enjoy the trip in on the local commuter train.

We can be certain there is signage for everything from shoe polish to travel agents, to coffee to soda pop as you make your way through the train tunnel or the underground parking garage.

You are greeted by more TV ads as your office elevator has a TV monitor inside. When you at last get to your desk, you begin to sift your way through multiple Newspapers and you barely glance at the belly-band ad on that new magazine.

Just as you exhale, Andy, you are bombarded with 117 e-mail messages and a host of on-line and social media messages that threaten to hold you hostage all day long.

Some you can turn off. Some are incessantly in front of you.
You take a few minutes at lunch to read the Newspaper and when you go for a coffee you read an article on your sports hero (or heroine) in the magazine someone left open in the kitchen.

Maybe you've got ten minutes to catch a breath of air and walk around the block, and see all the ads in the store windows and on garbage pails, and on taxicabs as they fly by, not to mention the street flyers and coupons being thrust at you.

You make a pit stop in the washroom before going back to your desk and there is signage in the bathroom in the stall door or beside the vanity mirror.

Returning to your desk you have 14 new e-mail messages, and often many of them are accompanied by an ad.

As you wind down the office day, you reverse the process and see the elevator and parking lot ads again.

On the way home, you want to work out the kinks and decide to hit the gym where there are more ads in the change-room, on sports bags and water bottles- heck even the sweatband has a logo promoting the manufacturer.

Fresh from the gym and shower Andy decides to pop into the local bookstore for a new book and you thumb through sports or dog Magazines looking for a new story and maybe you buy one or two titles.

As you leave the bookstore, you remember you're solo tonight, and decide to take in the latest George Clooney movie, and you're dwarfed by all the movie stuff in the lobby, then further held captive by the commercials running on Cinema Screen interspersed with all the new movie trailers.

Two hours and twelve minutes later, you leave the cinema and zip to any fast food chain for a 'healthy' burger. (You've just worked out after all) and you see all the restaurant signage, and it's written on the bag and the cup for your drink. You then detour a few minutes to the grocery store to pick up a few items for the next day and messages are everywhere.

On the door, the floor, the grocery cart, the aisle end displays, the shelf stickers, the divider on the conveyor belt before you pay.

As you at last arrive at home and the remaining strains of car Radio music fade away, you find the mail composed of a letter from your sister, a flyer for driveway paving, 2 new restaurants in the neighbourhood, a local accountant, the mechanic, a dry cleaner and a hospital charity lottery, as well as the community Newspaper that you'll ignore until the weekend.

Just when it appears safe to unwind with a drink in front of the TV you're inundated with a litany of commercials from furniture to pantyhose, and knife deals galore.....

....and somewhere in this continuous swirl of disjointed messaging that is in front of your customer everyday, **YOU have to stand out and say – I Am Here.**

You might remember that at the end of Media Spike #11, I noted an insurance company used only two media-at least in my experience- but I remember them because they were there constantly.

This is what you need to do in your media placement. When you've tested and tried and measured and know which media are working for you, then stay with them. Build the loyalty, trust, recognition, and consumer confidence by always being there.

You don't need to be in EVERY media. You just need to be in the one(s) which your target group will see regularly and respond to over time.

And you know which ones they are because you've been testing them..... Haven't you?

Stay tuned,

P.S. If you intend to be a long-term player in your industry, then treat your advertising like an ongoing marathon instead of a sprint.

Buyers like surety and confidence bred of ongoing presence and not a flash in the pan- digital or otherwise.

Media Spike #19 – A Knockout Blow

Thank you for coming back.

"It was a knockout blow. A punch so overwhelming that I didn't get back on my feet for 14 years. And to deliver a blow like that, they went to a lot of trouble."

So begins the international best seller Papillon© novel, by Henri Charrierre. His account, originally deemed a fantastic autobiography has been challenged for accuracy and more recently is considered a hybrid of his and other inmates experiences making it more a work of fiction. Regardless, it remains a masterpiece.

His opening line, like any good ad, was a powerful attention getter.

What was the 'knockout blow?
How hard did you get hit to be knocked out for 14 years?
Who are the 'they' that delivered such a crushing punch.?

This is the kind of memorable impact and recognition advertisers would 'kill for'.

They go to great lengths and enormous expense to put a message, which delivers a lukewarm response, anemic sales, and fails to build any brand awareness or excitement.

Before you spend a dime with me – I hope you do of course- but long before that, I want you to look at some advertising history:

David Ogilvy: http://www.copyblogger.com/lessons-from-david-ogilvy/

John Caples: http://www.lawrencecreaghan.ca/Archive/JohnCaples.htm

Victor Schwab: http://www.infomarketingblog.com/100-good-advertising-headlines-victor-schwab/

These three links will give you a glimpse into the thinking and strategies used by these three giants of the industry. Their ads are legendary. Their strategies are repeatable. Their results are irrefutable.

Smart writers and strategists who learned, early on, that the only way to make the ads work is if you get people to read them. To do this you have to stand out. You need to make IMPACT immediately. The best way to do that is with a Powerful Headline. Provocative. Engaging. Must See. Exclusivity. Provoke curiosity. Appeal to their interests. You need the headline to pull them to the next line. Then the next, etc.

Please remember that the headline is carrying the freight of your ad.

Probably as much as 80% of the success of your ad relies on the headline being interesting or provocative enough to get the reader to read the next line, then the next and so on.

When the time comes for placing your ads, I will spend your budget very efficiently. Saving you money, and delivering some tried and true and new media combinations to maximize the visibility of your message.

But all my efforts are in vain if your ad fails to get anyone to read it. Or watch it. Or listen to it.

While Mr. Charrierre was not writing an ad when he composed Papillon©, he was clearly provoking awareness. Creating interest. Stimulating desire. Initiating action.

That powerful opening line was enough to hook me into his 300+ page turner. He got my attention, and the attention of thousands of other readers around the world. Talk about a knockout opening line.

Believe me, no-one has more interest in seeing you invest in advertising space and time than yours truly. But it pains me to create a wonderful media stage of excellent players, platforms and media opportunities to highlight an ad, which was not going to raise an eyebrow.

Just because 80% of your budget should go to media placement, I am equally interested in the remaining 20% being used to full creative advantage as well.

Please click all of these three links to open a world of powerful ad history that has stood the test of time and will certainly bolster your future communications.

Don't worry, I'll still be here after you've read them and together we can put your best ads in the best places to be seen and acted on.

Here are those links again.

David Ogilvy: http://www.copyblogger.com/lessons-from-david-ogilvy/

John Caples: http://www.lawrencecreaghan.ca/Archive/JohnCaples.htm

Victor Schwab: http://www.infomarketingblog.com/100-good-advertising-headlines-victor-schwab/

Several readers of first drafts said, this is great Dennis. Umm- do you have anything from someone who's still alive?

Point taken.

Please let me introduce you to Mr. Andy Owen.
http://www.andyowencopyandcreative.com/

A Direct Mail copywriter veteran who has been writing ads as long as I've been buying them.

In his legendary 'Copycat' articles, he crafts a memorable effort here on the impact and persuasiveness of a good headline.

http://www.andyowencopyandcreative.com/pdfs/how_to_write_powerful_headlines.pdf

Stay tuned,

P.S. Did you STOP yet? Way back in article Media Spike #7, we encouraged you to stop advertising if they're not working. If your ads have **no STOPPING POWER, then please, Stop Running Them!**

Media Spike #20 – Be Sure To Send Your Question In the Form Of A Question

Oh good, you've come back. Nice to see you again.

By now you've gathered I take my media planning buying and role very seriously.

There is a lot of behind the scenes work in creative and production and media planning departments before any campaign makes it to the media.

But once it's out there, 'on the page' (or other media), then you've put all your eggs in that particular basket. Buying the space is the last stop before the campaign reaches the point of no return.

It does not go unnoticed by this writer that each media is different to different people. And my services, while all in the same portfolio of media planning and buying, are delivered in unique combinations to each client as required.

I am not the same agency to each client. Their needs vary, so my skill set and experience are adapted to deliver best solutions.

Sometimes that takes the form of:

• Doing just the research and a '30,000 Foot' overview of opportunities.

• Maybe it's taking it to a planning stage where I go more in-depth with each considered media option and deliver a recommendation, but no negotiations have taken place.

• Some clients will engage me to do the above as well as complete the negotiations and the buy just for Radio and Outdoor since they have a Print or On-line buyer housed elsewhere.

• Sometimes, it is the full package of planning, buying, scheduling a multi-media campaign, managing media payments and post campaign summaries and reconciliations.

• On occasion I am brought in to work on just one project to help out while the regular planner/buyer is overworked or unavailable.

Like you, my services are customised to the user, and my experience brings you talent you can count on.

Did you see this one?
One of my favourite mailings showing Two Options for your media planning.

This scored a direct hit with many readers because it identified the specific challenges and obligations they would take on by doing it themselves.

The worst is over for you now, right?
All you should have to do for your next
ad campaign is pick from
Option 1 or Option 2.

Today's Date

Media Spike Reader
125 Main Street
Found Nearly Everywhere
Your Home Town

Option # 1

Once you've set your ad budget for this year, the
rest is easy right? All you have to do now is contact:

- The Newspapers (Dailies, Commuter, Community)
- The Radio Stations (Local, multi-markets)
- The Television Stations (Local, National, Specialty)
- The Outdoor Advertising Companies
- The Magazine Sales Reps (Trade and Consumer Magazines)
- The Internet Sales Teams (and your web designer?)
- Conduct research for audience identification
- What stations to buy and why, and wrestle if you should use these three magazines or that newspaper and radio station.
- Contact all the print media for Tearsheets (proof the ads ran)
- Contact the broadcast media for affidavits proving the ads ran when they said they did
- Deal with the ongoing phone, fax (?), e-mail follow-up from everybody who wants to be part of the plan, and to answer everyone who isn't part of it.
- Promotional Contacts and Contest Options
- Find a Creative Team for what you want to say
- Contact a production crew to help you make the ads to the right sizes, specs and timing.
- Decide what size ad(s) you want –and why- and where and when they should start appearing
- Make sure the ads don't come out before the product is on the shelves

- You get to burn the midnight oil negotiating.
- Call the family or spouse and say you'll be late again.

OR

Option # 2

Call Us First
(905-427-3819)

Have an experienced
media professional deliver
all of Option #1
(and more) without paying
any more than it costs to
do it yourself.
(Maybe even less!!)

Call Us First, then go
see your family again.

Your Advertising.
Well Planned.
Well Spent.

Dennis Kelly
President
First Impressions Media
dennis@firstimpressionsmedia.ca
Ph & Fax: 905-427-3819

FIRSTIMPRESSIONSMEDIA.CA

I think this worked so well as it resonated so intensely with many clients who want their campaigns to be powerful, and think it stops and starts with creative.

It was a bold reminder that once they say yes to the creative message, there's a lot more they hadn't counted on to get in front of the right audience.
(You can tell it's a bit dated as I mentioned 'Fax' as a prominent media of the day. But the message remains unchanged.)

So as our series continues, we will offer up this opportunity for your consideration.

What would you like me to write about?
A particular media challenge?
A brief How To on purchase and placement of ad space?
Where should we advertise?

In our response, we will be as thorough as we're able and share your question and our answer with all readers. To protect identities, but to ensure I do provide authenticity, your initials and your city will be the only acknowledgement posted as the source of the question.

Sound good? I hope so?

Tell me what you'd like written about? How can I help?

Stay tuned,

P.S. Watch this...when you actually begin to formulate the question and write it down, you will often reveal to yourself the very answer you're looking for. See for yourself. Ask me a media question. Before it gets to me, I'll bet you have a clearer idea already what needs to be done. Self-discovery is amazing.

Welcome to Checkpoint Number Two

A summary of our second wave of 10 more Media Spikes, together.

#11: Marketing messages are everywhere. Consumers have short memories. Keep marketing all the time. In order to Stand Out, Be OUTSTANDING!

#12: Deliver your message with Impact. **Punctuate Your Point**

#13: What challenge are you solving for your client? How Can I Help You Today?

#14: There's too much money at stake to rely on 'gut' or a 'hunch'. Test your ads. Remember with Testing there is No Failure- only Results

#15: People love to be communicated to in different ways. When you've tested your ads, and see what's working, use multiple media mixes to be in front of your target group as regularly as possible.

#16: Television remains among the most dominant and influential media choices available. It is constantly being reinvented and refreshed, but it still commands mass audiences in a world filled with niche targets.

#17: A world of communications at our fingertips- Thank You for staying connected with me!

#18: The relentless barrage on our senses with media everywhere makes it a greater challenge to be recognized. When you've found a media- or multiples- which work, stay there constantly until they stop working.

#19: Your headline is carrying the bulk of your ad. If that doesn't attract your candidates, then the best media placement ever is moot if no-one reads the message. Create Stopping Power!

#20: There's a lot of behind the scenes work to make any campaign look easy. If you remember my clients' messages and pictures but don't recognize me, then I've done my job very well.

Once again it continues to be my privilege to be welcomed into your day. Thank you for your continued interest and support. The Media Spikes will resume their standard delivery pattern. Don't hesitate to send me any media questions. I'll do my best in response.

Thank you. I look forward to hearing from you.

Stay tuned,

Media Spike #21 – Practice is How You Learn What Works,
Or Doesn't…Just Like Testing

Welcome. It's always a treat to have your eyeballs meet my page.

At this writing, much of my city and all the local golf courses lie sleeping under a cold blanket of white snow. Very pretty, but handcuffing for my golf game.

Do you like to golf, dear reader?

I do, but be assured the players on tour are not losing any sleep with me out there.

I just marvel at how they squeeze so much out of every club.

Knowing what club to use depending on distance to the green, the weather, the wind, and their position on the scoreboard. Should it be a high lob from 87 yards with a pitching wedge to a pin tucked in the back corner of the green? Or is it a low pitch and run with a seven iron designed to maximize roll a better choice?

The reason they're on Tour and I'm writing is Testing. You might call it practice.

They are out there everyday when no-one sees them. Driving. Putting. Chipping. Short game. Long drives. From the bunker. From the edge of the water. From a downhill lie. Ball above the feet. Below the feet. Hook it around a tree. Out of the rough. In sunshine. In wind. In rain. There are no off-days to testing.

And all of this testing in all kinds of weather so that when it counts- when they are in the closing holes of a tournament, they know what they can do. They know how each shot will perform and they can trust what each club will do because they've been Testing.

One of my favourite golfers is Mr. Mike Weir. A fellow Canadian, and a fellow left-handed golfer. He was the toast of the nation when he won The Masters™ Golf tournament in 2003.

More recently he has struggled, but his persistence, perseverance, tenacity, and diligence is paying off as he is seeing a slow return to his winning form.

Your campaign should be like that too. Always out there attracting clients. Testing what works. Treating failures as learnings. Trying new media. Trying different approaches/shots to see what delivers the best results.

When you see what works best, set that as your benchmark. Then keep trying to top it.

Even when Mr. Weir is struggling, his worst game will always be better than my best game.

Because he has already established a level of excellence few golfers achieve- winning a Major- and he knows what it took to get there, and he's working hard to get back there.

Don't be afraid to experiment in your advertising. Continually testing is how you discover what works best and just like the pros, you know you can count on it when the pressure is on.

Stay tuned,

P.S. Want to know why your ad campaign is closer to golf than you think? Then you'll want to join me on the next message.

Media Spike #22 – Next Time You Want To Make A Sale – Go Golfing!

You're here again- How fabulous. Let's go.

In articles 16 and 21, we made references to golf in our media commentary.

While the sport is a favourite among people in the advertising and marketing industry - on both buying and selling sides, it also strikes me as a wonderful analogy for using different media as you would use different golf clubs.

You are allowed fourteen (14) clubs in your golf bag. Each one is designed to deliver a particular shot, the delivery of said shot is more in the control of the golfer than it is of the club.

Not unlike your campaign where the results you achieve will be equal to the skill you use in managing your media choices.

In simplest terms, let's pursue the analogy this way:
The Golf Ball is Your Message- Your Creative.
The Hole on the Green is Your Target Group - Customer-Buyer.

So how are you going to get your message in front of your customers as efficiently and with as much panache as possible? This is where your media planner/buyer earns their keep.

Just as in golf, there is no single right answer in your media mix.

You may have the great fortune of once in a while firing an ACE.
A hole in one.
Congratulations when that happens.

In the majority, it will take several well-executed shots with a selection of clubs to do the job.

Just as every golfer has their strengths- some guys can bomb it off the tee, while others have won tournaments just on the skills of their putting- your ad campaign has to draw on the strengths of each media you select.

Importantly, these can be used in many combinations. For example, today we're promoting New Home Carpeting available at Andy's – our favourite National Carpet Warehouse.

> Our media mix is structured not unlike how you use a Driver, followed by a 5 iron, then a pitching wedge, and finally a putter, which will determine your success on each hole.

Today, our campaign for **New Carpeting** for your home kicks off with a booming Driver launch off the Tee with a bold, intrusive 30 second **Television** spot airing on network television.

Long and straight, 285 yards down the fairway, this TV spot delivers the WOW factor as a multitude of consumers marvel at how big and bold you are. (They may not all be carpet buyers, but you've let EVERYONE know what you offer.)

While you're walking/or driving down the fairway, your TV campaign is still airing.
You're planning your next shot. Probably a 5 iron shot, 155 yards to an elevated green.
This is perhaps a **Radio** campaign which gives you an extended reach of the TV campaign, and allows you to keep it on the fairway with a New Carpeting message tightened to several major markets. Now you can be a bit more selective in the Radio stations you appear on, to be reaching your target of Adults 35+, Homeowner with $75K+ HHI (HouseHold Income)

Building on the awareness you have initiated with these two broadcast media, you want to get on the green with a 16 yard pitching wedge shot in the form of very specific home/shelter/lifestyle **Magazines** which will give you the visual extension from TV, plus put the message right in their hands. Here you have a chance for a more personal sales message, and provide detail to make the final push.

Sometimes that Pitch Shot goes in the hole- you made the sale right there. Kudos.
Most times, with practice and testing, that pitch comes to rest a few feet or inches from the hole.

Now comes the most valuable shot of all. Your Putter. You want to close the sale. You took them from the WOW of TV, to the local interest of Radio, to the personal excitement of Magazines and now they are THIS close to purchase and……….

….in our next Spike we'll show how we wrap this up so you finish on Par, and complete the sale.

Stay tuned,

P.S. The best score recorded for a single round of golf- 18 holes, is a score of 59. A total of six different golfers have recorded this between 1977 and 2013. The pars varied from 70, 71 and 72 strokes. Thus shooting 11, 12, or 13 under par is a memorable round for any golfer.

Media Spike #23 – Bringing It Home

Thanks so much for coming back, I've missed you.

Are your palms getting sweaty?

Heart beating faster?

Knees knocking?

Relax, it's a five-foot putt. You can make this with your eyes closed. You've been practicing and testing what finishes the sale so this is a cinch.

And as you grip the putter a little tighter, complete the backswing without breaking your wrists you're making the final sale with …

…..*Newspapers, or a Direct Mail Flyer, or a Coupon, or taking action on a Website, or a Referral from a friend.* …..and any and all of those can be the final stroke that completes the sale.

High Fives all around. You made par.

Every client responds differently to every message in every media.

To suggest only one media as the final lynchpin is foolhardy at best and irresponsible by me at worst.

There is no panacea. No Magic Bullet. No one single trigger to pull which completes the sale.

There is no one-way to make a putt. Every player brings their own style, and putting routine that works for them. Your campaign should do the same. Keep testing till you find what works for you.

If that disappoints you, it shouldn't. We all have our own reasons for choosing everything from carpeting to shoes to golf clubs, to steak, to housing, to every item that comes into your life.

Why would we delude ourselves that one size, one answer, one media fits all?

It's possible and probable that more than one media is responsible. And they all contribute to the sale. Which one is the tipping point will change with each consumer.

But you'll increase your opportunities to close the sale by having multiple media players keeping you on the consumers' fairway.

So we come full circle to the power of Testing. Practicing. Trial. Learning. Improving. As we expressed at the end of article Media Spike #14, the persistent testing allows you to fail small to win big. Works in golf. Works in media.

Stay tuned,

P.S. The beauty of this is that all media combinations can be tested. Campaigns can be of any media mix you like.

TV does not have to be National.
Newspapers can be powerful allies at any stage.
Magazines can carry an entire campaign on their own.
Digital media are being integrated into seemingly every campaign.
Outdoor advertising is a powerful solo player as well as a strong
supporting media to a host of other initiatives.

P.P.S. To demonstrate the versatility of each media, just like your golf clubs,
I borrowed this tip from the legendary Black Knight – golfer Gary Player.
When I'm off the green, but no obstacles in the way, I often use my Driver
as a putter.

It has the biggest, flattest face of any club. It gives me more muscle than I can get with a putter, and is safer than lofting the ball in the air with a pitching wedge. It has worked very well on many occasions for me.

Media Spike #24 – Let's Take This Outside

You're here. Perfect. Let's get started.

Let's take this outside was historically an invitation or taunt to move Outdoors for the start or continuation of a fight. I may want to bust my opponents jaw, but don't want to damage the furniture.

In a less confrontational strategy, let's take your advertising Outside.

I've always loved Outdoor advertising. Both as a planner/buyer, as well as a consumer. The necessary brevity to convey a powerful message with a visual and a few – stress 'few' – well chosen words is the ultimate impact.

Did you see this one? I've liked this one a long time and is perhaps the benchmark for me of Outdoor impact.

Some years ago, circa 1984, one skin cream manufacturer ran a wonderful campaign, pictured here, to demonstrate their implied benefit.

Our animated hero is sunburned red, and in the process of diving off a swimming pool diving board into a jar of their product. The only word was the Brand name on the jar. The implied message of instant sunburn relief was all that was needed. That's one reason I love Outdoor advertising.

Brand: Noxzema™
(Owned by Noxell at posting time, Now Unilever)

Agency: Ambrose, Carr, DeForest & Linton

Poster Company: Mediacom – Now OUTFront Media

Importantly for you and maybe your next campaign, is you can use Outdoor either as a lead media or in the supporting cast.

- It adds visual impact of your creative message.
- It can be an extension of a TV or magazine campaign with the same visual.
- It can feature a website or 1-800 Number as a call to action.
- It is very efficient and available in various formats depending on the market.

- Horizontal paper posters (10' High X 20' Wide) can capture a diverse audience being posted at high traffic arteries.
- Vertical Transit Shelters (4' Wide X 6' High) have a street-level presence reaching both vehicular and pedestrian traffic.
- Both of these formats are typically rotated to new locations after 4 weeks to deliver greater city coverage and increase reach.

Two trends are emerging you may want to consider.

Many standard poster locations are now moving to Digital Formats. Your ad is still a skyline dominant image of 10 feet X 20 feet, BUT, now that it's electronic, you can change the creative more frequently without incurring new printing costs.

Here's how it works. If the nature of your product /service offers seasonal variations, then you can have one creative that offers hot chocolate and soup on a wintry day, and a cool beverage and sandwich when the sun is shining. Because you can change the file electronically, you save a lot on printing costs.

The transition to this format varies from market to market, but ask your Outdoor supplier to tell you if this is an option for you.

The second changeover we see happening is the redevelopment of many downtown cores. This means that oversized superboards, posters, wall murals are being removed...and not being replaced.

To counter this, many smart advertisers have adopted, or enhanced their use of Exterior Transit advertising. Signage on the sides, and backs of buses and streetcars. It ensures your message is very mobile, it reaches both pedestrian and vehicular traffic and generates recall, which matches or exceeds that of other Outdoor media formats.

Don't you just love an endless buffet of media choices?

Stay tuned,

P.S. We offer a series of articles on Outdoor Advertising you may find of some assistance. The following link will take you there:

http://firstimpressionsmedia.ca/how-to-improve-your-advertising-using-Outdoor-media---a-10-part-series.html

Media Spike #25 – The Best Part Of My Job

Greetings once again.

Do you like your job?

I hope so. You spend so much of your life at your work, you really should enjoy your work.

Yes I know, commutes, low pay, lousy bosses, belligerent co-workers, and a host of other strains can make your day to day a continual nightmare. You have my empathy.

In the majority, I'm lucky enough to say I still enjoy my job.

For me, there is enormous satisfaction in crafting a smart and creative media plan which saves my clients money, points them in a new direction, stimulates sales, drives traffic, elevates their profile, and just plain makes them achieve their sales objectives.

Media Planning and Buying - It's not rocket science, nor brain surgery, but being the steward of your ad budget is a responsibility I take very seriously. I like to see your campaigns do exceedingly well. Knowing that my efforts helped make the cash register ring for you, that's a great reward.

So how do you improve your advertising without immersing yourself into multiple years of planning and buying experience?

Genuinely you are already head and shoulders above 90% of your competition just by staying with me this long. No false modesty, but the tips and insights revealed thus far are strategies that have worked for me for 3 decades for dozens and dozens of large and small clients. They will work for you.

In fact, one of the strongest resources you have is the first document that got you started with me.

If you haven't already accessed it, you can download your own copy of the

Spike of Angels 57 Spikes Media Planning Guide & Template by clicking here

This single document, when completed by you, will give you and your marketing team some necessary direction and compel you to focus on what you want the campaign to do.

By itself, this document, in various forms through the years, has saved hundreds of thousands of dollars for many clients. It reduces or eliminates guesswork and assumptions, and it helps the client and agency to be literally on the same page. Nobody likes surprises, especially when money is concerned.

Today, like my Outdoor ads...Brevity is best.

Stay tuned,

P.S. Is it time to abandon ship?

Media Spike #26 — Hurry, hurry now, get out while you can, please hurr…

Welcome, get inside quickly.

The sky is falling!!!
The sky is falling on all traditional media.
Get out while you can.

So one panicked industry colleague warned.

Traditional Media — you know the kind, Radio and Television, and that printed stuff like Newspapers and Magazines- all Toast. Oh and don't even get me started on Outdoor. They are all going the way of the dinosaur.

Such dire warnings have been sounding for the past decade and longer.

Perhaps instead of the Chicken Little panic button, we acknowledge the evolution of media vehicles, the changes in technology, the proliferation of Social Media channels, and the changes in consumer tastes, demands, and capabilities.

There is no question the 'Internet' has long ago eclipsed 'in its infancy stage' and now is a major player in local and global communications.

What disturbs me is the sudden desperate abandonment of the tried and true and successful media en masse, in favour of a multi-faceted vehicle, which is spinning off madly in all directions.

History is littered with 'the next thing' which was supposed to cannibalize everything that preceded it.

A brief timeline:

When Mr. Johannes Gutenburg made his first **Printing Press** in 1450, it revolutionized communication as multiple copies of news and information could be spread faster. **Newspapers** would begin to arrive in earnest through the next century.

When Mr. Samuel Morse sent the first **Telegraph** in 1844, traditionalists of the day feared all print messages would be lost to this newfangled wireless technology that relied on dots and dashes.

When Mr. Guglielmo Marconi had Transatlantic signal success in 1901 with what would become **Radio,** pundits at that time feared print and telegraph would be rendered obsolete.

Electronic **Television** was first successfully demonstrated in San Francisco on Sept. 7, 1927. The system was designed by Mr. Philo Taylor Farnsworth, a 21-year-old inventor. He had lived in a house without electricity until he was 14. But full-scale commercial television broadcasting did not begin in the United States until 1947.

The mid 1950's- deemed the Golden Age of **Television**, became the foundation for advertisers and networks to ultimately reach a nearly global audience. The prevailing attitude became one of scoffing at all those archaic pioneer media who came before them.

Sitting in the weeds was the development of technology that would lead to the launch of the **Personal Computer** as a mass-market consumer electronic device in 1977.

Clearly this new device was going to obliterate everything in its path and there would soon be no need for print as we'd have a paperless office. Certainly no need for Magazines and TV's and Radios since the 'Personal' computer was the composite of all these vehicles and more.

Today, more than 550 years since Mr. Gutenburg's printing press success, you can still print a copy of this page, or thousands of others- right on your own desk. Or simply store it digitally forever....until the next technological revolution.

Hmmm? Does this mean- The More Things Change, the more they stay the same?

Because even that expression has multiple rebirths since it was first used by French novelist Alphonse Karr, in French. The original wording is: "Plus ça change, plus c'est la même chose." Attributed to circa 1850.

Is there more?

Stay tuned,

P.S. No it is not time to abandon ship. Nor do we need to start bailing- we are not taking on water. Rather these new social media venues- personal, professional, grapevines, 'Dear Diary on Steroids', have given passive consumers a voice beyond all historic proportion.

The Goliath of media and advertising is behaving as it's always done, adapting to the tools and talents of its age.

Media Spike #27 – The Game Remains The Same

Hi, thanks for coming today.

Recently one reader W.M., asked, *So Dennis, are you suggesting that we dig in our heels and resist change? Are you closing your eyes to the platform that is the Internet?*

Well formed and valid questions.

To the first, no I am not for a moment suggesting we resist change. It is the only constant, and all our efforts to stop the tide will only have us swept up in the undertow. Change is necessary. It disturbs complacency and challenges us to get more out of ourselves, and our communication.

To the second, my eyes have been keenly adjusted to the Internet as a media platform for over a decade with different clients experimenting (Testing) different messages and delivery styles.

But ultimately it is still Marketing. The tools change, and we change to better use the tools we created. But human nature being what it is, we all crave communication, and ideas, and content, and useful information.

The Internet and the digital age have ushered in instantaneous communication. In a heartbeat, a message, which once was a feature ad in National Newspapers, is now delivered to only one neighbourhood, or globally with unmatched speed and precision to an on-line audience who see it on a host of stationary, or mobile media tools.

My contention, and I'm pleased to say, multiple clients have concurred, is to introduce these new elements to our ad campaigns with a 'let's give it a try and TEST IT' approach rather than abandon everything that got us to this point.

If you've been testing your creative and your media mix as you go along, then these new components are part of the normal integration and they have to prove their worth in delivering sales. (Not likes, or retweets etc., but actually get down to a measurable and useful metric- SALES.)

I work with several clients who care less if they are liked, but have a huge passion for how many SALES- how many units of product did we move as a result of the last campaign.

It strikes me that advertisers who integrate 'Social Media' into their campaigns need to do so with a recognition that historical sales strategies don't play as well in this environment.

The messages today need to be informational, educational, and supportive to the customer buying process so that the customers get to know and like and trust you before you begin offering a sales message.

Incidentally, when you are prepared to offer up a sales message - beyond just education - this is the time to move them from the social media forum to your website. Now they are on your turf.

By way of analogy, when Television was in its infancy late 1940's early 1950's, networks recruited performers, entertainers, personalities from that 'old' media, Radio, to help them get underway.

No less a powerhouse name than Vaudeville and Radio personality, Mr. Milton Berle, was the lynchpin to the commercial success of this fledgling new media, Television.

Initially warmly received, revered, idolized and known as Mr. Television, the tool, which had invented him, was rapidly transitioning as audiences were looking for new and different entertainment.

Change was so rapid in TV, that only a few short years after 'Uncle Miltie' ruled the airwaves on Tuesday nights, he was supplanted by other programming.

So too with the Internet and social media. The early successful models are giving way to new methods of interaction with consumers. They are not dismissing all previous methods of contact, and most of those should remain a part of the mix.

But the message from advertisers needs to reflect the new reality of consumer engagement.

Expect a longer courting process (back to my dating plan strategy unveiled in article Media Spike #3) on line to win more hearts and wallets with a longer term relationship build.

Such is the start of a customer for life - the best you can hope for.

Stay tuned,

P.S. Keep testing. Keep practicing. New messages. New Media. Create the hybrid mix that works for you.

Media Spike #28 - Absolute Heresy They Cry, The Nerve of Adding a New Media, Why I Ought To..

Welcome aboard.

A couple of weeks ago, back in article Media Spike #15, I spoke of the importance and relevance of having multiple media touchpoints for recognition. You might also recollect A Day in the Life of article Media Spike #18 on the diversity and omnipresence of media vehicles. Most recently we shared our analogy of media vehicles and golf, in article Media Spike #22.

Tell me dear reader, have you only ever had the same dinner, every day, forever?

One likes to hope not. Change. Variety. Diversity, are keys to health, life, happiness and media.

Introduce new players one at a time to see how well they work. Keep the ones that do. Discard the ones that don't.

In several references thus far in this series, I've noted how one insurance firm used only two media, but they were there all the time. They had done their testing, and these media prevailed and were a foundation of their ongoing marketing efforts.

Several advertisers have plowed forward by sheer brawn of their budgets. They just bought more of whatever media they were using. While it dwarfed the competition- until budget ran out- it just overwhelmed their target group beyond saturation point and failed to expand their geography long term because too many funds were tied up in one media.

I grant there is merit in having a strong leading media. However, I would suggest you never have a reliance on any one media for any product or service.

Many On-line purists were startled they had been delisted from the G-man of On-line due to algorithm changes or an unintended hiccup.

More than one client has put everything into a Newspaper campaign just as the union goes on strike for three weeks. One United Kingdom client had the misfortune of bankrolling his TV campaign to start on the day of Princess Diana's tragic car accident, and his campaign was nowhere to be seen in the melee of news reports on the tragedy.

That's a lot of eggs in any one basket.

A minimum of two media is preferred, and five, eight, ten media at a time will certainly help to keep you consistently top of mind.

Sure Dennis, but does it work? How much difference does it make by adding a secondary media? Well, let's take a look.

To this point in our series, we've only touched on Magazines intermittently. So let's give them some deserved attention.

Many advertisers have relied on Television as their sole media.
It has doubtless worked for many of them, as it continues to be a vital part of their messaging strategy. Good for them.

So what happens when you suggest....*Instead of buying 100% TV, let's consider spending 75% in TV and the remaining 25% in Magazines?*

Study after study, survey after survey, results from 14 aggregated Return on Investment (ROI) studies validate the power of Magazines to drive purchase decisions* (Magazines Canada – Consumer Magazine Factbook 2013 Page 116)

If Television is our base at 100%, then the addition of On-Line ads raised the index between 101% and 114%.

The addition of Magazines to TV and OnLine raised the index between 160% & 175%. This is just in their ability to drive purchase decision.

Magazines demonstrated their great impact of addition to the mix where their biggest influence is felt in Brand Imagery and Purchase Intent at 91% and 81% respectively. *Higher than each of TV and Internet.*

No less a name than Meredith Corporation™, a prominent magazine publisher, headquartered in DesMoines, Iowa, USA, created a program to prove advertising with their brands (Magazine titles) guarantees a direct increase in sales. After one year, in several product categories, participating advertisers realized an average return of $7.81 return for every dollar spent on ads in their Magazines.
THAT's 781% Return!!!
The Power of Print cannot be overstated.

Would you consider it beneficial to spend the same and increase sales? Then you'll appreciate this experience.

The Dutch based firm Unilever proved this 'multiplier effect' as they changed spending from 100% TV to 75% TV and 25% Magazine and saw a 6% increase in sales volume.

(The above results are all available for confirmation from this same Magazines Canada Consumer Fact Book 2013 as referenced above.)

If you're already combining media to further your awareness and increase sales, you have my applause.

If you're still waffling, then test it for yourself. You will be pleasantly surprised at the results, especially when they show up on the bottom line.

Stay tuned,

Media Spike #29 -
Half Time, Starting the Back Nine, There's Still More To Come

Hello again, come on in.

Can you believe we are half-way there already?

Seems we only just got a chance to say hello a short time ago and we're halfway through our Fifty-Seven Media Spikes.

Are you enjoying them?

If you're still with me till now I'll take that as a yes.

A few questions have surfaced from readers to date so now's a good time to exhale and respond.

R.A.F. writes... Where did the Media Spikes name come from? Is it somehow significant for you?

Thanks R.A.F., Media Spike comes from a variation of my Blog: The Spike of Angels
http://www.firstimpressionsmedia.ca/the-spike-of-angels-blog.html

I believe your ad message should have the impact and staying power of a Railway Spike driven into the frozen ground. Immovable. Yet it should be served up with the sensitivity and grace of Angels.

Each of these messages to date imparts one more Spike in my epistle to you that communications should be delivered in a multitude of formats. Each one able to stand alone, but when used together, an unbreakable link to build a campaign or nation. Thank you RAF

Hey Dennis, writes K.K., what's up with the 57 Media Spikes? How did you arrive at that number?

In a lucky twist of fortune, those are the last two digits of my birth year, and at this writing, I will have been on this planet for that many years. So one Spike for every year seemed a good target. Thanks K.K.

Tell me Dennis, asks T.C., if we like what we've seen so far, do you have any other resources we can take a look at?

Thank you for asking T.C. As a matter of fact, several readers have already explored some of the links provided to my website for articles on

Radio advertising
(http://firstimpressionsmedia.ca/how-to-improve-your-advertising-using-Radio---a-10-part-series.html)

and my series on **Outdoor** media
(http://firstimpressionsmedia.ca/how-to-improve-your-advertising-using-Outdoor-media---a-10-part-series.html)

and some readers have also learned I offer a downloadable PDF e-book which distills my 30 years into a guide book of <u>Nine (9) Media Secrets</u>. Regularly priced at $197, this practical hands-on How To Guide is worth multiple times that asking price. In keeping with the spirit of numbers, it's now available for **$30 in keeping with my 30 years** in the Media Trenches. I think, and of course hope you'll like this one. **30 Years for $30. Incredible Value and Content**

At this writing, it is available exclusively through this First Impressions Media website link. Don't delay. Act now to dramatically improve your advertising. That's 9 Secrets of How To Improve Your Advertising

http://www.firstimpressionsmedia.ca/online-store--start-with-9-secrets---.html

M.L.S. asks, Why have you stayed with this business so long? Aren't there other things you'd like to do?

A great question MLS and I stay in this role because I'm seldom if ever bored. I genuinely still like my work. I love being able to present a solution to a client, which spends their funds smartly and creatively and bolsters their profile. I get a lot of satisfaction in turning a blank sheet into a creative plan.

I can't think of another industry or job, which would have given me exposure to so many other industries.

I've been privileged to work with many fine professionals on accounts including, hotels and trucks and financial services, plus computer printers and carpeting, workboots and medical services, not to forget cameras and beer, and chicken and florists, as well as several charitable causes, and travel and provincial and federal government accounts.

Also in my portfolio is planning and placement for a variety of automobiles and auto parts and a host of others have kept me sharp and interested. And I love bringing that daily enthusiasm to your doorstep.

Thanks M.L.S. I still like what I do for 'work!'

Stay tuned,

P.S. Several years back, the legendary golfer, Mr. Jack Nicklaus lent his name and image for the endorsement of American Express™. Looking into the camera he poses a question to the effect of ...*Do You Know Me?*

Seemingly a rhetorical question as his golf fame appeared to make him worldly recognizable. But perhaps, some people who don't follow golf may not have known him, hence the question.

It was a great attention getting strategy and made me wonder. If we don't often know the face or talent behind the scenes, does that make their work or accomplishment any less valuable?

I pose this because one reader recently asked,
...So Dennis, what have you done? Like how would we recognize your work? How would we evaluate you? Fair enough.

Let me answer that this way.

I know that nobody wakes up Monday morning saying '....where can I find a good media person...', especially when my role is typically behind the scenes.

If I introduced myself to you at your office with a professional introduction - spoken or written which goes:

Hello - my name is Dennis Kelly of First Impressions Media.
If you engage my services, you'll immediately have access to my 30 years experience of smart media planning, and efficient negotiations which has raised the profile of many campaigns in all media, and saved thousands of dollars for dozens of clients in multiple industries.

You might smile politely and say, That's nice, Dennis.

If however, my introduction went:

Do you know me?
My name is Dennis Kelly of First Impressions Media.
If you don't recognize my name, then I've done my job.

But chances are better that you'll recognize my work.
My role made it possible for you to see ad campaigns from multiple clients including these on the following pages, and many other fine brands.

- **Canon Canada – Printers & Photographic Products and Canon Business Solutions**

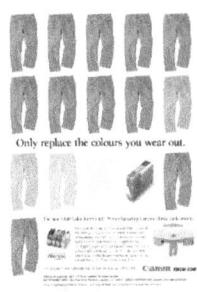

Canon Canada
Agency: Lackey Communications
Ad: Jeans for Printer
Creative Director: Bruce MacDonald
Art Director: Angus Brimacombe
Media: Consumer Magazines
Timing: 1998

Canon Canada
Agency: Lackey Communications
Ad: Elvis Stojko for Elph Camera
Creative Director: David Purser
Art Director: Angus Brimacombe
Media: Outdoor Transit Shelters
Timing: 1999

Canon Business Solutions
Agency: MacDonald-Kerr Partnership
Ad: Your Business. Your Canon.
Creative Director: Bruce MacDonald
Art Director: Tony Kerr
Media: Magazines & Transit Shelters
Timing: 2001

- **Yamaha Canada Music**

Yamaha Canada Music
Agency: First Impressions Media
Ad: Keyboard for Christmas
Creative Director: Angus Brimacombe
Media: Newspapers
Timing: 2003

- **Chicken Farmers of Ontario**

Chicken Farmers of Ontario
Agency: 13AD
Ad: Savour More Flavour
Creative Director: Angus Brimacombe
Media: Consumer Magazines & Transit Shelters
Timing: 2010

- **City of Toronto – Livegreen**

City of Toronto
Agency: Agency 59
Ad: Livegreen – Conserve Energy
Creative Director: Brian Howlett
Media: Rickshaws (and Radio)
Timing: 2008

- **Heart & Stroke Foundation of Ontario**

Heart & Stroke Foundation of Ontario
Agency: Agency
Ad: Yoga
Creative Director: Brian Howlett
Media: Print & On-Line
Timing: 2012

• TICO - Travel Industry Council of Ontario

• Cosmo Music

Travel Industry Council of Ontario (TICO)
Agency: Larter Advertising (The Marketing Garage)
Ad: Look Before You Book
Creative Director: Rob Worling
Media: Commuter Train Car Wrap

Timing: 2013

COSMO Music
Agency: Larter Advertising (TMG)
Ad: Come Out & Play
Creative Director: Rob Worling
Media: Train Station Pillars

Timing: 2011

• Timberland Workboots

Timberland
Agency: Larter Advertising (The Marketing Garage)
Ad: Take Shelter Inside
Creative Director: Timberland
Media: Outdoor Posters

Timing: 2014

Timberland
Agency: Larter Advertising (TMG)
Ad: The Original Yellow Boot
Creative Director: Timberland
Media: Outdoor Posters

Timing: 2014

Timberland™: Canadian Agency - The Marketing Garage. Two Campaigns.
Locations- Multiple Major Canadian Markets. Timing: Fall 2014.
(Planned & Placed Outdoor, Television and Radio campaigns for Timberland on Behalf
of Larter Advertising/The Marketing Garage from 2009-2014)

Many of the preceding campaigns had sister versions in TV, on Radio, On-Line, on Buses etc.

This list is not meant to be exhaustive, but merely to show that as a Media Planner/Buyer, I have very little to do with the ad you see, but I have everything to do with you being able to see it.

Media Spike #30 - You Don't Need To Be An Artist To Be Creative

Greetings!

Are you creative?

If you don't mind me asking can you Sing? Draw? Paint? Dance? Compose? or have a flair with any of the multitude of art forms?

Accept my most appreciative applause of your talents, if you do.

I'm always impressed by anyone who possesses these skills, which elude me. One of my brothers is an accomplished amateur musician who still has expertise I long for, but I fear will remain out of reach.

I ask because two decades ago, one of the Creative Directors at the agency I was with posed that same question to our entire Media Department of ten or so people.

When only a handful of hands were raised - including mine - he admonished us for not understanding that we are ALL Creative. For some it's more easily manifest in impressive works of art. For others, in the grace of dance. Still others can command a room with their vocal expertise, and yes, us media people too.

The creativity comes from starting with a multitude of random items, objects, events and opportunities out there, and molding them into a powerful, compelling platform which showcases the client's product in a new or innovative or provocative way.

Think Different. Think Outside The Box. Break the Rules.

Start somewhere new unexpectedly.

Change it up. Something new you should try.

Advertise on the **TOP** of trucks to reach people in office buildings. Get your name at multiple high-end Golf Courses to reach a more affluent decision-maker.

GAIN   AWARENESS   BY   BEING DIFFERENT ON PURPOSE.

When the times comes for you to advertise, and it will – BE BOLD- DISTINGUISH YOURSELF- **CREATE SOME PIZZAZZ. (That means attractive and exciting vitality and not more Pizza's)**

But while we're on that topic, I had one client use exactly that tactic. For one of their promotions, we had a digest page size, 4 colour flyer, produced and attached to all Home Delivered Pizzas in one market for one month. These were affixed to the top of the delivery box.

It's not parting the Red Sea, or breaking the sound barrier, but it was distinctive for them to break a mold as a more staid advertiser, and launched them to a whole new audience. The response to the flyer was very positive and the return on investment more than justified the expense of this novel approach.

Capitalize on opportunities as they come up. They can be unexpected goldmines and show your client and their customers you are thinking.

In one memorable effort, a Front Page Banner position of the National Newspaper came available.

That **NEVER** Happens (or at least in 32 years for me, it happened once)

We presented this opportunity to the client, understanding we would be in rotation with other advertisers and appear every 8th day for one year. THE CLIENT LOVED IT. It was a spend in excess of six figures, but the exposure, the brand recognition and the resulting sales made it worthwhile.

A series of five or six ads were done, all in Newspaper Banner format. Full page width, about 2" high.

One ad featured a very intense looking, bald, black male, who was tattooed on shoulder, neck and side of face. Beside him read the Line: Not for Everyone. Next to that was a client product picture. Beside that were the words: This Is.

Other ads in the series were along the same line of 'Individuality'. We all have different tastes in everything. Some items have a better chance of appealing to a wider audience than others.

This creative was DIFFERENT. It drew praise from multiple places and importantly helped trigger sales.

Certainly this was a client who had the resources to take advantage of this. But I would not have brought it forward if I didn't think they had the funds for it.

Being creative doesn't mean it has to be zany, or wacky – because you send lots of the wrong messages with those tactics too. But it does have to show a distinctive and relevant way of showing off.

Whichever media mix you choose, let their strengths and inherent creativity help you make the sale.

Stay tuned,

P.S. Defining creativity (I personally liken it to being resourceful with the items you have all around you)

That teachable skill, creativity, has been defined in many ways. It has been called

- A "mental *activity* performed in situations where there is no prior correct solution or answer" (*Encyclopedia of Creativity,* vol. 2, "Teaching Creativity")
- A "*process* of developing new, uncommon, or unique ideas"
- An *experience* of thinking "characterized by a high degree of innovation and originality, divergent thinking, and risk taking"
- The "*generation* of novel, useful ideas"

http://www.celt.iastate.edu/creativity/defining.html

Welcome To Checkpoint Number Three

A summary of 10 more Media Spikes, together.

Gosh the days are flying by aren't they? I hope you're enjoying these tips.

#21: In advertising parlance we express it as Testing. In any other sport we'd call it Practice. On Stage we'd call it Rehearsal. Your ads should always be injected with something new to see if they can continue to be improved on. That Grand Slam of success may be only one or two words away!

#22: Truly your advertising campaign is not unlike your golf game. The right media, just like the right clubs- and how you use them- make all the difference to your success making the 'green $$$$' or putting on the green. Use them in the right combination and you can avoid the rough.

#23: Remember to test on a small scale so you can see what will work on a grander scale. There is no panacea. No one size fits all. Every client, every campaign, every customer has their own style. Finding the media mix that pulls the trigger for the most candidates is what your testing is all about.

#24: The success of Outdoor advertising is measured by its impact using brevity. Space is at a premium. No place for long copy. Formats, facings and geographic placement can all drive increased response and traffic.

#25: Satisfaction of a job well done leads to wanting to do more just like it. Nearing the 1/2 way point in our series, you are head and shoulders above most competitors already!

#26: The media evolution continues. New technology is expected to cannibalize and obliterate all its predecessors. Funny thing is - most of them are still here. Because they have evolved too. Do not be a Chicken Little.

#27: The Internet is not going away. It has become such an indispensable part of the fabric of our global communications. But we continue to caution to not abandon all the media which brought you to this point. Test with On-line. It is a veritable goldmine of testing, with prompt results and will do in days what historically took weeks or longer. Test.

#28: Please do not put all your media eggs in one basket. Adding a secondary and third and fourth media will enhance your reach and memorability and just maybe....sales.

#29: At the half-way point now, we reveal how 57 Spikes was born, and provided a link to Nine Secrets.

Another link http://www.firstimpressionsmedia.ca/online-store--start-with-9-secrets---.html

will allow you to access and download our e-book with Nine (9) Secrets of How To Improve Your Advertising. This summarizes 30 years in the media trenches for $30, and gives you specific worksheets and assignments to help you improve your campaigns Just Like That!

#30: Be creative. Be Different. There is a world of **ME TOO!** Do something unexpected. Not bizarre as that sends the wrong message, but do something that helps your ad get noticed.

This is such a treat for me to be able to share these experiences and tips with you. I genuinely hope they are a good refreshing read for you and have offered some guidance for you.

Thank you for your continued interest and support. The Media Spikes will resume their standard delivery pattern. Once again, please don't hesitate to send me any media questions. I'll do my best in response.

Thank you. I look forward to hearing from you.

Stay tuned,

Media Spike #31 – Tell Them To Sell Them

Welcome.

Does it seem like most Magazines have had the diet many of us crave? They get thinner and thinner without even trying.

Diminishing ad revenues. More fierce competition. Everyday. Multi-media are making numerous Magazines desperate for business. Or forcing them to pack up the tent altogether.

And it's so unfair. Magazines will get people talking about you.

Did you know Magazines are the leading contributor to word of mouth recommendations?

Many advertisers like you feel their magazine ads aren't working.
So they stop advertising.

So the magazine gets thinner. So the magazine has a harder time selling because they're getting thinner. Advertisers don't want to use a thin magazine, so they stop advertising there. The circle is perpetuated. This is true in both trade and consumer Magazines.

Here's How You Fix This.

Create and run better ads. Your ad is your salesman. Remember our buddy John Kennedy and Salesmanship In Print. Give the customer solid, usable, real, genuine information.

Egos be damned, the customer cares little about your logo. Even less about how many awards you've won. They want information. Pretty pictures seldom drive the sale. They want to know:

How does it work?
Why is it better than what I'm using now?
What colours does it come in?
Is it guaranteed?
For how long?
Where are the technical specs? (at least some of them)
What problem are you solving?

(Incidentally, price is not the exclusive motivator for any product purchase. If you can show how you deliver a superior benefit(s), customers will pay a premium.)

Yes, it should be creatively delivered, but the integrity of the sales message has to be paramount. People are forgetful. Do you remember ANY of the estimated 3,000 (or 300) messages (Media Spike #11) that hit you today? You're competing with over an estimated 24,000 messages per week. Unless you've carved an identity by putting the client first, - solving their problems, your prospect turns the page.

Did you know at this writing the average cost for a full-page 4-colour ad in one of the Top 10 Canadian English Consumer Magazines is $29,428.80, averaging 502,000 circulation achieving an estimated 3,273,000 in readership?

How many units or models do you have to sell to pay for that ad? Maybe six, perhaps seventy-one, or five thousand? Make your ad the best salesman you've ever hired.

Tell your whole story. Imagine that this is the <u>ONLY</u> communication your prospect will ever see. This one ad of yours is your gospel. Are you forgotten with a flip of the page? That's an expensive way to sell. You may get pats on the back. (OR 'Likes' in today's vernacular) Ovations at award shows. Great. How many sales did it produce? Sales pay salaries. Did you give them what they wanted and needed, ***or did you just look good on the page?***

How Powerful is a Magazine? Ever heard of Rolls Royce? Mr. David Ogilvy, an ad genius, wrote factual, information-based ads for Rolls Royce. Arguably his most famous ad read: "At 60 miles an hour, the loudest noise in this new Rolls-Royce comes from the electric clock." This first appeared in 1958.

The implied benefit of impeccable engineering only escalated Rolls Royce sales and image for many years. The ad went on to highlight 19 specific facts that informed prospects of all that Rolls Royce has to offer. **The original ad ran in only two Magazines and two Newspapers. That's it.** And more than ½ century later, it remains legendary. **That's The Power of 26. Will your ads have the same impact and longevity?**

https://marchingagainstphilip.wordpress.com/2010/05/04/"at-60-miles-an-hour-the-loudest-noise-in-this-new-rolls-royce-comes-from-the-electric-clock"/

Okay Dennis, so this ad history stuff is kinda neat, but what else can I do, now that the whole world it seems has abandoned everything else in favour of Digital formats and the jungle of Social Media?

If you promise to come back tomorrow, I'll tell you, and I'll save you a spot - right where you are.

Stay tuned,

Media Spike #32 – Five Steps To Improve Your Ads

So pleased you could join me,

KABOOM!

Perfect. Now that I have your attention, that's exactly what your ads should do. Jolt me from my sleep, clear off the haze, and make me pay attention to what you are saying.

Too many ads lack the Pizzazz of Spike #30, but get half of that right with lots of ZZZZZ's

Ever read a good book? By any author. What did they do? They kept your attention. The narrative was so vivid as to pull you in to its pages. The pace accelerating, then pausing and keeping you riveted.
THAT's what your ads need to do. Regardless of the media. Your ads needs to be Interesting. Exciting.
Grab you by the lapels and take you along for the ride. Your ad can't be too long-only too boring

Five Steps to Improve Your Ads

1. Why are you advertising? Not just blindly throwing bucks out there. Take the time to write out why. What do you have to say, and will you make it interesting and informative to your buyers?

Whether you do it yourself, or through your agency, write out all the things that your product or service does. Please do this without pictures or images. No-one knows your product like you do. Even if you're not a professional writer, write out what your product/service does. You'll discover some powerful gems that maybe you take for granted, but are the buried treasure for your prospects.

2. Stress the Benefits. Not just 'Better Service' which is too subjective, but actually write out the features of your product. Then express it as a benefit that will be attractive to your customers and prospects

> • Our Reinforced Impact Driver delivers longer lasting performance due to increased battery charge so your down time is reduced.

> • Our stocks have shown consistent short and long term growth due to our diligent research and careful investments, thus raising the value of your portfolio every year.

Pick one compelling benefit. Your signature benefit which catapults you ahead of the competition, and hang your hat on it. You can use multiple benefits of information, as subsets of your headline as Mr. Ogilvy did. Pick something that is a worthwhile benefit and a drawing card that attracts your audience.

3. When you place your ads, regardless of the magazine(s) you choose, please, please, **please TEST the ad.** Before you spend a boatload on a huge campaign, test the ad on a small scale to see if people are responding to it. The more you test, the more you will continue to improve your sales. It can be a coupon. A 1-800#, a Call to action to direct them to your website. Promise them and deliver them something when they respond. Not some vague idea of effectiveness, but actual measurement to show return on investment. TEST Your Ad.

4. Be Choosy. Remember that each Magazine caters to a different audience, age, dynamic, gender, interest group. Use the 'halo' effect of a positive Magazine to bask in its implied endorsement. Do not always be swayed by the lowest price. Several Magazines may command higher pricing, but that should be reflected in the calibre of audience they reach. The paper stock and the imagery and their total circulation are key factors. By the way, don't buy JUST based on circulation. Many Magazines have great numbers, but they are padded, or their readers may not be your target group. Volume does not always beget accuracy.

5. Be creative. Not just in your messaging - although that's important. But have some fun within the Magazine. Here's a tidbit to keep you from overspending - The only 'Premium Positions' for any magazine are the covers. Usually only 3 of those are sold for ad space: Inside Front, Inside Back and Outside Back. Sometimes, Centre Spread- DPS (Double Page Spread ads are available, depending on the binding format of the magazine.)

Study after study, showed that once you are inside the magazine, every page enjoys the same level of readership and attention. Most advertisers continue to seek out, 'Well Forward, Right Hand Page' as the Holy Grail for maximum readership.

IF, IF, you can have your ad appear adjacent to, or within a relevant article or editorial, that won't hurt your cause. But the statistical average is, all inside pages are equal.

In addition, please remember You are not obligated to run full pages. (I acknowledge some Magazines do limit themselves to only full pages or at worst, full and half-pages only).

Remember, you are always testing, so experiment to see what helps you stand out.

• Use the Magazines to run 3 consecutive right hand page 1/3rd vertical strips.

• Use it as a carrier for your insert or flyer (try to be 2nd or later in the polybag to save money)

• If you have multiple Magazines, stagger the insertions over alternating months. You'll stay in market and in the audience mindset, but you'll stretch your budget.

• See if you can get a regional edition instead of National. It will save your costs if you don't purchase unnecessary geographic coverage.

• If there is a Reader Reply Card appearing in the magazine for you or anyone else, try to be the ad page where the Reply Card is bound in. The typical heavier stock of the Reader Reply Card will have the magazine fall open to your ad, gaining you a first glimpse from the reader at no extra charge.

• Make sure you see and approve the magazine(s) BEFORE you place your ad. Please take the time to do this. I've witnessed too many apathetic or half-hearted efforts by marketers who should know better.

Then they whine after it's printed when it was literally in their hands ahead of time and could have been corrected. It's time well spent. Get a hands - on look at the Magazine environment where you will be featured.

• Consider that just maybe it's the only piece of marketing a prospect ever sees from you, make sure you can be proud of it.

The Power of 26 is Word Play at its simplest, and its most powerful.

Put all that marketing muscle into your Magazine ads, and you'll hear them talking about you, all the way to the cash register.

Stay tuned,

P.S. What did Mr. Ogilvy say was the #1 Most Important Decision?

Mr. Ogilvy wrote: #1: The Most Important Decision: We have learned that the effect of your advertising on your sales depends more on this decision than on any other. ***How should you position your product?***

Should you position Schweppes as a soft drink – or as a mixer?
Should you position Dove as a product for dry skin or as a product which really gets your hands clean?

The results of your campaign depend less on how we write your advertising than how your product is positioned. It follows that positioning should be decided before the advertising is created. Research can help. Look before you leap.

http://www.infomarketingblog.com/ogilvy-mather-direct-ad-4-how-to-create-advertising-that-sells/

Media Spike #33 – How Can I Help You Today?

Hello again.

How Can I Help You Today?

When was the last time - if ever - you received a Cold Call with such an offer?

What's bugging you?

What do you need that's going to relieve some of your pain?

I extend this offer exclusively to my readers who have made it this far along with me because you've demonstrated some loyalty, and interest in my work, so I'll try to give something back for your time.

The moon and the stars and jewelery, riches and automobiles, have already been claimed by my wife and family.

So beyond those trinkets, **How** can I help you today?

Contact me now by e-mail at: **dennis@spike33.ca**
(This address is exclusive to you as a Book Reader.
It appears nowhere else.)

I'll do my best.

Have a great day and please,....

...Stay tuned,

Media Spike #34 – Exactly What I've Been Saying

Oh good, you're here.

Are you shivering from all those Cold-Calls?

If you've ever called 100 people a week, only to get voice mail, hang-ups, or rude prospects then you know it's a brutal way to get your message out there.

Even setting an appointment with people who don't really want or need to see you can be tough slogging.

Yet thousands of professionals of all stripes continue this daily ritual in the hope of striking on 'exactly' the right day when the prospect needs just what you're selling. I wince at the odds.

If you continue to do this, I applaud your tenacity.

While it is not a forte of mine, I do respect Cold-Calling. If done properly, it can be a very powerful lead generator.

If you'd like to learn or polish your skills in this area, there is no-one better than **Wendy Weiss**, the Queen of Cold Calling. To find out more, click this link

http://www.coldcallingresults.com/

Certainly like any communication effort, if it works for you and is delivering results and sales at a price point that is efficient for you, then by all means continue.

I do encourage you though to consider multiple means of sales.
Test small to learn big.

You don't think so?

This e-mail series did EXACTLY that. By the time you get to today's message, there may be tens or hundreds or thousands of readers who have absorbed this type. Lucky me if that's the case.

BUT at the very outset, I tested small. It was sent to seven (7), yes seven people. Contacts in Toronto, Canada, the United Kingdom and Florida, United States to TEST if it was working.

And you know what? It WASN'T!!

There was a hiccup in the original link that was to take you to the PDF for your first download.

If you were to come along now, hundreds or thousands of readers later, and I didn't know it wasn't working, imagine how sloppy that makes me look. Rather diminishes my prospects I'd say.

By Testing small, I was able to isolate and fix the problem before my recipient list grew to the enviable size it is now. That's how every ad of yours should earn its stripes. Being marketplace tested.

Stay tuned,

Media Spike #35 - It Costs HOW MUCH?

Thank you for coming back.

Maybe this year you're considering some advertising to boost your image and stimulate sales. How fabulous. I certainly wish you every success.

If any tips I've shared so far have been of assistance, I'm glad to have been of help. If I can do more, I'll be glad for that too.

Starting with a new slate is wonderfully exciting and intimidating all at once.

You can't wait to 'Get Out There' until you learn **how much** is out there, AND How Much It Costs!!

NO KIDDING. Staggering isn't it? The cost of media space, in nearly all media can be very crippling and more than one company has rolled the dice and not recouped the investment. That hurts.

Others, like one client of mine several years back, dropped $100K (yes one hundred thousand dollars) on a Special 2 page Newspaper ad in a major market paper with a circulation of ¾ million copies.
A reasonably efficient $133 cost per thousand (CPM) for a Powerful hit.

I can remember a time when that kind of money would have bought you several baseball players, for more than one season, not just one ad.

Regardless of the generation, advertising is not an inexpensive proposition. If it is done well, with smart, creative, thoughtful, relevant ads, with a usable message which resonates with your target group, then you can enjoy a wonderful return on investment.

How do we get there?

Well if you've been noticing, we've dropped a few hints along the way about Testing. When you see empirically what's been working, then you know you can refine and confine your spending to just those media which are consistently producing results for you.

The costs of media are always going to be a going concern for small, medium and large businesses.

As your universe grows, you tend to want to attract more customers. Meaning casting the net wider and further a field.

To do that well, often means incorporating more extensive and more expensive media options, which tell your sales story to more listeners, viewers, and readers.

Price does not tell the whole story. EVER. It is certainly a factor, but if you buy exclusively on price, you certainly cheat yourself out of reaching some very worthy candidates for your products or services.

Contrary to a wide held belief, many customers DO NOT buy based just on price. If that were true, there would only be one style of car, one style of boot etc.

For the next few Media Spikes, we will speak to the costs associated with several media players.

As an opening effort, we will look to Social Media, which has the grandest bandwagon ever.

Certainly the Internet has opened many new doors for advertisers of all sizes to communicate a message one to one, and is often substantially less expensive than other media options.

Although I wonder sometimes just how much is saved.

The savings derived by more modest space cost for Social Media options are somewhat mitigated by the necessity to have personnel constantly monitoring and responding to your customers. The cost is now in staff (yours or your agency's) and customer service follow-up expenditures and less in purchase of an ad unit.

Is **Social Media** truly the advertising saviour many are touting it to be?

Well, like everything else in marketing – IT DEPENDS.
> On what you want to do?
> Who you want to reach?
> What sort of message do you want to share with them?
> Are you prepared to devote the time to develop a relationship?

The proliferation of Social Media is global. A hugely daunting double edge sword for the enormity of reach potential, tempered by the obligation of sustaining a dialogue – multiple times per day, to create a relationship with them, to encourage them to try and buy your product or service.

Happily for this writer, some Testing has already been done.

Done on a modest scale and time compressed, it can't be construed as truly scientific. Nevertheless it serves as a barometer, a microcosm, of the options and challenges within all Social Media Channels to date.

In March 2013, Mr. Christopher Null conducted this specific test.

It was entitled **Do Social Media Ads Really Work? We Put Them To The Test.**

This was reported on in TechHive.com. (a link appears later in this article)
Mr. Null conducted a campaign, which was mimicked in five (5) Social Media channels:
Google Adwords, Facebook, LinkedIn, Twitter and StumbleUpon.

Varying formats, and price points preclude an exact match, but as near an equal measure as possible was used and the results are worth noting. The following italicized type is verbatim from Mr. Null's article.

- *Facebook ads appear particularly ineffective at getting clicks, possibly because users have already become accustomed to ignoring these ad placements due to their location. Experiment with low CPC bids on Facebook when getting your feet wet.*
- *LinkedIn is easily the most expensive service on which to advertise, and clickthrough rates are low.*
- *Twitter's almost 1 percent clickthrough rate is double the rate of AdWords, and far and away the best I encountered. Ads are surprisingly cheap. It's difficult to target your ads on Twitter, but they still appear effective despite this limitation. Perhaps that's because promoted tweets are virtually impossible for users to ignore.*
- *StumbleUpon is a great option for extremely inexpensive ads, and if you are targeting a broad swath of consumers, it's definitely worth a look. If you're sold on social media advertising, consider these tips before you begin.*

- *Start small. Set a very low budget for a CPC (not CPM) ad, and let it run for as long as you can to get a sense of how it's performing. Tweak the ad frequently and track your results. Some services let you run multiple versions of the same ad, so you can compare results among them.*
- *Clicks aren't everything. Despite getting hundreds of clicks over hundreds of thousands of impressions, my business didn't net any new clients from these ads. Understand what value your clicks actually bring to you, and make sure your ROI is positive after you have sufficient history to examine.*
- *Think about your target market. It's an old adage that "Twitter is for business" and "Facebook is for fun." My experimental results bore this out, so think carefully about what social networks your potential customers are likely to be using before charging ahead.*

To see Mr. Null's entire article and testing, please click this link:
http://www.techhive.com/article/2030740/do-social-media-ads-really-work-we-put-them-to-the-test-.html?page=2

Does this mean Social Media isn't working? **No.**

Does it mean you should not try Social Media in your communications? **No.**

What it does mean is that like all its predecessors and traditional counterparts, your advertising should be tested to see what's working.

Perhaps you'll have a staggeringly successful campaign with a mix of one Social Media platform coupled with Radio and Outdoor media.

Maybe the breakthrough comes with Social Media ads on Mobile Devices while the target group is in the Mall seeing a Mall Poster ad and a store flyer.

As I suggested earlier in this book, I would suggest no more a reliance on any one media than a reliance on any one golf club to play the entire round.

What I would suggest is that you use all the social media platforms as leverage and drive traffic to your website where customers are on your turf and you can educate, inform and sell them better.

Your ads are a bit like employees. *"If you pay peanuts, you get monkeys." –Sir James Goldsmith*

Don't always opt for the 'cheapest' option, because you know what type of respondent you'll attract.

Stay tuned,

Media Spike #36 – Well, Did It Work Yet?

Greetings dear reader.

So did you buy it yet?

That new suit? The watch? The sexy earrings? The new car? The sweater? The carpeting?

C'mon, the ad has been out there for 3 days now, why aren't you running to the cash register? Most advertisers will stall and hem and haw about what they want to say in their ads.

Then when they at last pull the trigger for an On-Line or Radio, or Newspaper, or Outdoor, or Television, or Magazine or a composite of all of these in a campaign, they're startled when the cash register doesn't light up within minutes.

Typically, most consumers receive their product information a spoonful at a time. Learning a bit more about you with each exposure. They may not want or need you right away, but when they do, you want to be the one they think of.

Can you remember a particular product you saw advertised and RIGHT AWAY ran out to buy it?

It may have caught your <u>A</u>ttention. But you're not impressed enough yet.

The second time it caught your attention and piqued your <u>I</u>nterest enough to learn more.

The next time in front of you, it caught attention, held interest, created <u>D</u>esire, but not action.

The following two, or five or thirty more repetitions continued until finally all elements of the **AIDA** formula came together and you took some <u>A</u>ction and purchased the product.

As advertisers, the sale can't happen fast enough.
As consumers we're not always in such a hurry for the purchase.

Thus repetition becomes necessary to overcome resistance until finally we agree to part with their asking price.

That repetition comes in multiple forms and we can see this same advertiser in Newspaper and Radio, or in On-line and Magazine, Television and Outdoor, Radio and On-line, in-store and in elevators and all the time you are driving sales and building the brand.

Personally, I believe if you are driving sales successfully, and making your customers happy with dependable, reliable service and products, the brand building will take care of itself.

Your name or logo will transcend all hesitation and speculation because your sales efforts and follow-up have earned you a trustworthy reputation. Something that many brands fail to achieve because of inconsistency.

Do you remember what I mentioned way back in Media Spike #3, that's about six weeks ago now, that your advertising should be like an ongoing dating process.

That was true then and it still is now. My wife agreed to our first date all those years ago, but I'm still trying to woo her and keep her attention and interest because the Brand is ME.

Remember you are trying to cultivate a long-term relationship with your customer. They are your bread and butter and need constant attention to keep coming back to you for whatever your service is.

Another key point to remember in your advertising and marketing is that YOU will tire of your message and media mix long before the customer does.

Too often clients have pulled campaigns that were still working simply because the 'agency' wanted to freshen it up. **BUT it's still working**. If it ain't broke, don't fix it. This is a key finding from your Testing - you are still testing aren't you?

The testing will show you what message is working in what media and if one ad starts to falter, then try another, and another. Keep something going all the time and as well as you're able, always be in front of your audience with some messaging.

You may not be persuaded on the first attempt, but multiple exposures will lead to enhanced opportunity to make the sale. Maybe you only needed 3 exposures while your neighbour needed 19. As long as it continues to pull in sales at a respectable pace, then keep your messaging in the marketplace.

Stay tuned,

Media Spike #37 – Our Initial Message

Thank you for sharing a few minutes with me.

You may have noticed several Media Spikes so far have mentioned The Power of 26.

An expression I've coined and use as a subtitle in my Blog as part of my Spike of Angels Blog.

http://www.firstimpressionsmedia.ca/the-spike-of-angels-blog.html

Quite simply The Power of 26 refers to the enormous power in the alphabet, and how those 26 letters are the lynchpin to our world and every level of communication.

And sometimes, in media presentations, you've probably noticed a lot of abbreviations and initials are used to take the place of cumbersome words and titles.

While texting and tweeting have forced us to rely on phonetics instead of full words, I thought it might be helpful to elaborate on many of the initials and short forms you may see or hear or read in many media memos.

A Glossary of Media Terms could fill the next five to six e-mails in this series. That's more than overwhelming.

But I thought a few terms from each of the primary media might be of assistance. This is not meant to be exhaustive, but to give you some knowledge next time these terms show up in a media presentation. (You'll impress the media person too, if you know some of the jargon.)

ADJACENCY: A commercial time slot immediately before or after a specific program (First spot when the program goes to break, or last spot before the commercial break returns to programming.) If these two spots are the same advertisers, it's often called **Bookends.**

Audience Composition: The characteristics which make up your target group. Based on demographics, lifestyle, income, education etc.

BCR-Budget Control Report: Sometimes monthly, quarterly or annually, it tracks actual expenditures versus projections.

CA: Census Agglomeration: A geographical area, defined by Statistics Canada, with a population of between 10,000 and 99,999.

CMA - Census Metropolitan Area (CMA): Geographical Area defined by Statistics Canada, with a population in excess of 100,000.

CMA – Central Market Area (CMA): Geographical area defined by BBM, usually centered around one urban centre.

CPR – Cost Per Rating: The costs of delivering a message to 1% of a pre-determined group.

CPM – Cost Per Thousand: The cost to deliver a message to 1,000 individuals-preferably the individuals who fit your target group.

CUME - Cumulative Audience: This is the total unduplicated number of homes or individuals who are reached by a schedule of commercials or programs or print issues within a given time.

EFFICIENCY: Evaluating how a good a buy you or your space buyer did based on CPM's or CPR's as above.

EMA – Extended Market Area (EMA) Geographical area comprised of a market and adjacent counties or census divisions as defined by Nielsen Media Research.

FREQUENCY: The number of times an advertising message has been exposed to a target audience.

GRP's - Gross Rating Points: The sum of all ratings delivered by a given schedule against a pre-determined target group. GRP's= Reach X Frequency
(Reach ie: 25%, times Frequency, say 4 times = 100 GRP's)

HUT -Homes Using Television: The percentage of households with one or more televisions tuned in at a given time.

IMPRESSIONS/MESSAGES: The total number of commercial occasions (or ads) scheduled, multiplied by the total target audience potentially exposed to each occasion. The media plan's impressions are usually expressed as Gross Impressions. That is the total potential number of opportunities for the message to be seen.

Pre-Buy Analysis: A report of the estimated deliveries of a purchased media schedule.

Post Buy Analysis: An analysis of actual media deliveries calculated after a spot or schedule has run.

REACH: A measurement of the cumulative unduplicated target audience potentially exposed once or more to a particular program, station or publication in a specific time period. This is usually expressed as a percentage of the target population in a geographically defined area.

There are easily over 200 additional terms of Jargon and alphabet soup related to the industry and to Media in particular.

As noted, this was not intended to be exhaustive - nobody wants to read a dictionary - but they may give you a glimmer of familiarity that will make future meetings and presentations clearer for you.

The Power of 26 is an indispensable tool for every interest and industry. In the abbreviated words of my son's good buddy 'Tigger' of Winnie the Pooh fame, T.T.F.N. (not a media term, but Ta Ta For Now!)

Stay tuned,

P.S. The explosive growth of Digital Advertising and Marketing has amplified the acronyms glossary substantially. This little media book will grown enormously to accommodate the inclusion of all abbreviations.

To save you time and me pages, I invite you to check out an excellent summation of Acronyms and their explanations provided by HubSpot Blogs at this address:

http://blog.hubspot.com/marketing/marketing-acronym-glossary

Media Spike #38 – What Do You Know About What You Know?

Here's a question for you.

Are you a problem solver?

Do you have an expertise that provides a solution other people could benefit from?

Of course you do. You're an expert gardener, dog trainer, computer programmer, social media marketer, advertising sales rep, dentist, florist, teacher, banker, and in all those capacities and thousands more, you have solutions to a multitude of problems and challenges faced around your neighbourhood and the globe.

You've been doing this for years and you've become quite good at it.
But you've been going to 'work' for 8 years and you know your job backwards and forwards. You could do this in your sleep.

It seems so easy….and it is…because in the majority, you have devoted experience, time, training to get to the expertise you have now.

But because **YOU** do it everyday, it doesn't seem that special to you anymore. Heck if I can do it, anyone can do it. Or so goes the self-deprecating commentary.

BUT YOU have amassed _enormous knowledge_, talent, expertise and you can solve problems that perplex thousands of others. This is EXACTLY what advertisers are doing. (and you can too!)

I would venture to say dear reader, that if you're a good banker, there are thousands of people who would love to know what you know to improve their financial situation.

Many large and small companies continue to offer their expertise in the form of products, or services we see and use everyday.

Maybe you will use cereal or toast or mouthwash everyday. Those manufacturers have sustained their presence in multiple media to make sure you're not forgetting them and always put them in your grocery cart when shopping.

Maybe you need to see your dentist two or three times per year. His (or her) expertise is in demand and especially prized when you're in pain.

Chances are, you won't see them advertising in the same channels as your mouthwash provider.

But they likewise have the need to market themselves as a Pain Reliever.

Perhaps this is among the biggest challenges companies face and that is, who can best use their expertise on an ongoing basis and how can we best position (see Mr. Ogilvy- P.S. of Media Spike #32) ourselves to be the solution to their problem.

Importantly, it will in all likelihood, take more than one media channel to reach them on an ongoing basis. Which channels, well that's where the continual testing comes in to play.

Many advertisers have used one media as a stepping-stone to the next. Starting with local Newspapers, then local Radio, then regional Magazines, then a larger Newspaper ad, plus they add another Radio station, then they jump to local Television – you know - to try it out, and when that's worked, they invest more in bigger TV and Outdoor campaigns ....and we applaud these behemoth corporations who grew from nothing to Omnipresence seemingly overnight.

In fact, as smart problem solvers like you, they have recognized the service they are delivering relieves pain or delivers pleasure. They are bringing that expertise to wider and wider audiences and they have been testing all along to see what is working and what they can discard.

But what's happened here? Why are they growing the way there are?

Because, they have taken the time to understand the commonality of their audience. They used the media, which consistently, persistently and efficiently reach them, and deliver the triggers which cause their audience to purchase.

They have learned what works and what doesn't. They have discarded or minimized the underperforming media and put their dollars into vehicles which deliver positive Return on Investment, and they continue to put their muscle behind them.

Remember please, not everyone uses every product in the same way or for the same reason or motivation. We are all different. But we all have some commonality that compels us to use mouthwash (I hope so anyway!)

Remember, the knowledge you have should be put to use in your media planning. You should have some presence of your expertise in front of your customers and prospects on an ongoing basis. It gets harder to be forgotten or dismissed when you are in contact with your customers everyday. After all Dear Reader, you're a problem solver.

Stay tuned,

P.S. Earlier in this series I've mentioned the importance – especially when you're starting out- of picking one media and testing it to see how well it works.
Then replace or enhance as necessary.
Ideally you want to have more than one marketing vehicle out there at any time.

If you needed some reinforcement to that idea, you may want to take a peek at this article by Mary Ellen Tribby.

http://maryellentribby.com/stop-focusing-on-one-channel-of-marketing-at-a-time/

Media Spike #39 – It Costs HOW MUCH? – Part 2

Hi again.

Forgive me, I nearly forgot.

Recently one reader reminded me I hadn't spoken about the costs of media as much as I promised to a few e-mails ago.

Thanks to B.K. for that memory jog.

It Costs HOW MUCH?!?

Well if it costs that much we don't want it.

Regrettably a refrain I heard from one client on several occasions earlier in my career.

Amazing how funds go from: The Sky's the Limit, to, We Have to Save Budget.

The arrival of more electronic media platforms does not diminish that there will still be some costs to your ad campaign. Else why are you advertising?

But as clients we are all guilty of wanting to spend only $12 and get $100,000 worth of exposure. As though it is somehow the 'Media's fault prices are so high and why can't we knock 90% of those costs off in negotiations.'

Despite sometimes wonderfully positive media negotiations, and great savings, there remains the reality of the media costs. Perhaps you're among many clients who are startled to learn your ad budget doesn't buy as much as you hoped or expected.

You may recollect in several earlier Media Spikes, we made several golf analogies.

Each club performs based on the skill level of the user, but also understanding there are some clubs better suited to a specific shot than others. So too with media.

So which media is suited to which situation? What you want to do and how much you can afford are key drivers to your media choices.

Wanting to dominate the Outdoor skyline with powerful backlit posters for 3 months is wonderful.

But if you're spending is more modest at several thousand dollars, you're better off looking at media which won't exhaust your budget so quickly.

To demonstrate just what a consistent Ad Budget would do across all media, the following comparatives are presented.

Please bear in mind this is prior to any formal negotiations and I recognize additional factors come into play. But to get an idea of what one budget could do across different media, witness the following.

Using a Budget of $100,000, devoted to each media, in the major market of Toronto, Ontario, Canada, you could expect to buy:

Outdoor Media:

> 40 Paper Posters,
> Measuring 10' X 20', appearing for eight weeks,
> At a cost of $100,000

> 100 Transit Shelter faces
> Measuring 4' Wide X 6' High, appearing for eight weeks,
> At a cost of $100,000

> 20 Horizontal Backlights
> Measuring 10' X 20', appearing for eight weeks,
> Translucent Vinyl+
> At a cost of $100,000

Newspaper Media:

> Five (5), ½ page, 4 colour ads in Toronto Broadsheet Newspaper
> One ad per week for 5 weeks in Front News section
> Delivering estimated 2.4 Million Impressions to Adults 18+
> At a cost of $99,750

> Two (2) full page, 4 colour ads in Metro Edition of National
> Newspaper, running as
> One ad per week for two weeks in Metro Edition at a cost of
> $102,200

Magazines Media:

> Five (5), Full Page, 4 colour ads in Toronto specific and Toronto
> splits of National Magazines (General Interest category)
> Estimated 650,000 circulation @ 3 Readers Per Copy
> Delivering 1.95 Million Impressions to Toronto audience
> At a cost of $95,650

Television Media:

Two hundred & twenty three, Thirty second spots on one citywide station at 20+ spots per week for 10 weeks
To appear on a mixture of Prime (62%) and Off Prime programming
Delivering 11.1 Million Impressions to Adults 25-54
At a cost of $100,000

Radio Media:

480, 30 second spots on a prominent news station
Airing as 32 spots per week Reach Plans
Flight can run for 15 weeks.
Delivering 12.9 Million Impressions to Adults 18+
At a cost of $95,520

On-Line Media:

Leaderboards (728 X 90) and Big Boxes (300 X 250)
Using ten (10) geo-targeted websites
At an average $30 CPM (depending on unit and site)
30,000 Impressions per week, for 10 weeks, on 10 websites
Delivering 3 Million Impressions to Adults 18+
At a cost of $100,000

Please understand I know this is a simplification as many additional variables go into the final media selection. But I believe it's important that when making a huge decision of where to invest your media funds, you have every right to have an appreciation of what you are buying, and what you are getting.

Stay tuned,

Media Spike # 40 – Feelings Versus Facts

Glad you could make me part of your day.

Is your history hurting your future?

Do you want to try something new, but worried that what you remember isn't the way it is now?

We have talked about testing your media.

Gradually bringing change along to see how it works.
That does not mean an immediate abandonment of traditional ways for new.
But it doesn't mean not trying something new to you because you have an altered perception of reality.

Earlier today, I had a challenge with one client who wants to utilize a couple of websites to specifically reach Women age 35 -40, and they had to be equal spends to English and French audiences.

Two inherent challenges:
1) No woman out there will admit to being over age 35!!
2) There is - to my knowledge - no website that caters just to one age.

There is typically a range of 18-24, maybe 25-30, or 35-54 etc., so to isolate a site to a specific age is nigh impossible.

I did find a couple of extremely well targeted sites which fit the budget, timing, language, age range and gender with excellent precision.

The challenge came not from the empirical data, which substantiated the strength of the sites, but from the antiquated perception this client has about one of the sites.

It is the On-line version of one of the most internationally successful and recognizable publishing brands around the globe, and has been for nearly a century. Its readers are loyal, affluent audiences who are exactly who this client is targeting.

But the stigma of using a brand, which has a dated image in the client's mind, is preventing her from realizing just how refreshed and modern and relevant this site is.

Perhaps that is the important challenge and strength I bring to my role.

To the best of my ability, I'm wanting each media recommendation I make for you to be able to stand on its own numerical merit.

Not just, *I think, or I believe,* but rather hard, independent data - preferably 3rd party, which objectively and dispassionately displays the integrity of the chosen media and allows me to recommend media for their own sake and not because of my emotional attachment.

Are there favourites? Naturally. But there are many occasions when a Publication, Radio station, or Website is bumped from a plan because it does not meet the necessary criteria. It may otherwise be a fine choice but unless it can stand up to its competitors on its own merit, it will be replaced.

Our own reluctance for change, and for the recognition that the things we remember have changed, can often be our largest obstacles.

My client was carrying the vestiges of seeing this magazine in her youth, surmising it was an "old person's" magazine. Now that she's grown up, she still has that perception and is hesitant to use their new incarnations – both print and On-line.

What she's wrestling is the challenge of empirical data (substantiating this vehicle in print and On-line versions), that this publication is refreshed and more vibrant than ever, against her memories of this being an old person's magazine and can't be comfortable appearing where she thinks is outdated.

I certainly have every respect for the emotional attachments - good or bad - that we all have to certain events or media in our history.

As nice as those may be, the objectivity has to rule the day. If it can be demonstrated that this refreshed vehicle is the best ticket for you, then use it for all its worth.

If it can continue to be relevant and reach and influence the desired target audience efficiently and effectively, then keep using it if it ain't broke.

Stay tuned,

Welcome to Checkpoint Number Four

A summary of our fourth two weeks, and 10 more Media Spikes, together.

#30: Be creative. Be Different. There is a world of ME TOO! Do something unexpected. Not bizarre as that sends the wrong message, but do something that helps your ad get noticed.

#31: Magazines are the leading source of word of mouth recommendation. Use the power of print to capture attention and build sales.

#32: Remember five simple steps to improve your advertising:
1) Why Are You Advertising?
2) Stress the Benefits of Your Service.
3) TEST, and TEST and Keep TESTING your ads
4) Be Choosy about where you choose for your ads to appear
5) Be Creative. Look to opportunities within the pages of each magazine
   to STAND OUT.

#33: How Can I Help You Today? - e-mail me: dennis@spike33.ca and tell me how I can help.

#34: The coldest place in the world can be Cold Calling. If you must do it, please access http://www.coldcallingresults.com/and get help from Wendy Weiss - the Queen of Cold Calling

#35: Keep TESTING. The cost of advertising is huge today and price is always a factor. But it's not the only factor. We looked at Social Media testing done in March 2013 by Christopher Null. Not unlike all other media, the best direction is to start small. Test to see what's working and by the way - keep testing.

#36: Few sales are 'Instant'. It has taken time to nurture and grow that relationship for any one sales message in any media to be the trigger, which makes the sale.

As a seller, it can't happen soon enough. As a buyer, we're not in such a hurry. Be consistent. Refresh yourself occasionally, but keep the name out there and never stop marketing.

#37: Turning initials back into words. Demystifying some of those strange and cumbersome media terms and abbreviations. Remember, The Power of 26 is in Everything you say and write.

#38: Are you a problem solver? Of course you are. You have expertise in something that someone is looking for right now.

#39: It costs HOW MUCH? We presented six scenarios of how $100,000 could be deployed. Amazing to discover the same budget will buy so many different options!!

#40: Don't let your history compromise your future. Adapt to embrace the technology as it works for you, but do so gradually. If it ain't broke, don't try to fix it.

Gosh you have been busy. Keeping up with these tips everyday. I appreciate you taking the time. I hope they are of interest to you

Thank you for your continued interest and support. The Media Spikes will resume their standard delivery pattern. Once again, please don't hesitate to send me any media questions. As always, I'll do my best in response as quickly as I'm able.

Thank you. I look forward to hearing from you.

Stay tuned,

Media Spike # 41 – Are You Lost In Translation?

Welcome back.

Does the Media campaign sometimes get lost in translation?

Perhaps you've been the recipient of, or the deliverer of a proposal that goes a lot like this:

Dear Client,

• This campaign will launch with a 4 week Radio flight at a weekly 200 GRP's weight with a target objective of 40% Reach at a Five time Frequency.

This will cume to a 65% Reach at a 12.3 times frequency.
It will be skewed to affluent females aged 25-54 living in
urban centres with HHI of $75Kplus, and who are the
principal grocery shopper!

Usually after this slide a timid hand is raised with an almost sheepish question of **Ahem... excuse me sir, but what did you say?**

•**Jargon** Every industry has its own language that allows you to communicate quickly and efficiently with colleagues in your business. But to someone on the outside, a simple paragraph like the above may as well be Greek (or my personal nemesis - Calculus).

Technical Speak. There are a multitude of abbreviations, acronyms, and short forms in media that could make phone texting read like Shakespeare by comparison.

In a recent Media Spike (#37), we noted a number of Media Abbreviations and definitions for your reference.

We have reiterated a few of them here and show them in practical application.

• A few prominent terms occur regularly in ad planning and to help you get a better idea of what's going on, here are some explanations:

•   **Reach:**

This is a measurement of the cumulative unduplicated target audience potentially exposed one or more times to a particular program, station or publication in a given time frame. (How many different people in your defined target group could see   your   ad.)

Reach is usually expressed as a percentage of the target population in a defined area, or the impact your campaign will have against a defined audience.

IE: We expect to reach 33% of Men aged 18-24 with this campaign. This is also expressed as 33 Ratings as each rating is 1% point of the defined audience.

·Frequency:

This is a means of measuring the number of times your 'reached' audience will be exposed to the commercial in a stated period of time.

IE: Through the life of this one week campaign, our target group will hear our spot an average of 3.1 Times. Thus a 3.1 Frequency

·GRP's - Gross Rating Points:

This is the total of ratings achieved by a given schedule against a pre-determined target group.

This is calculated by multiplying your reach times your frequency.

We just said we had a campaign which 'reached' 33% of Men 18 - 24, and we reached them with a 3.1X Frequency.

Therefore our campaign delivered: 33 X 3.1 = 102.3 GRP's (Gross Rating Points) (as a benchmark, a 100 GRP Radio campaign is not uncommon.)

There are numerous permutations and combinations of media, and within each media, which can be used to help you create that lasting impression.

Mediaspeak

• So what did I say in the earlier paragraph? Anyone care to translate?

• Our intention is to run a 4-week Radio campaign in urban centres.

• Each week, we want to have reached 40% of our affluent female grocery shopper fives times.

• At the end of four weeks, we hope that 65% of our audience will have heard the message 12.3 times

• A good Media person should be able to walk you through the language they work in, but express it in terms you can understand.

Please bear in mind the above are just a few samples of the terminology you can expect to hear in many media presentations.

Do not EVER hesitate to ask for clarification. Most of us media people are bursting to give you every answer we can to help the education and improve your confidence in us.

Stay tuned,

Media Spike # 42 – Ladies & Gentlemen Mr. ELTON JOHN

A Vibrant Welcome as we dive into today's message.

A Keyboard of Fireworks

As explosive as a hair-triggered fireworks display, legendary performer Mr. Elton John (aka- Reginald Kenneth Dwight) was the epitome of flamboyance.

Outrageous glasses, and costumes. Sometimes funny, always colourful and an electrifying stage presence, he commanded attention....but when he began to play- he COMMANDED INTEREST.

For all his attention-getting stunts and visuals, he had the musical chops to back-up his stage presence with enormous singing, songwriter and piano playing talents.

He was an ad for HIMSELF everywhere he went.

Love him or hate him for his music, his relationships, his style, you can't help but marvel at his consistency of entertainment and talent to satisfy audiences again, and again and again from the 1970's to the present.

My question to you is simply- **Why Aren't You Doing The Same Thing?**

What? Hey Dennis- I'm no rock star? I wouldn't be caught dead wearing those outlandish outfits and besides I can't play piano like Elton.

You're absolutely right....and I can't either.

However, that doesn't mean your ads should be bland and lost in the crowd.
They should be distinctive. Have a recognizable signature of yours on them. Maintain continuity from ad to ad, media to media, year to year, so that your branding is always consistent.

Not unlike Mr. Elton, it can't hurt you to freshen up your look or add more SKU's (Stock Keeping Units) to your portfolio. Maybe not a new recording, but a new product or new service each month, or model year etc., to show your audience that you are still in there pitching.

Remember to change your headline frequently to see how well it's working and track what responses you're generating. Much as you are interested in developing and sustaining a great image, your ads should be designed and implemented for SALES.

Try this: Invest $100,000 in your salesman.
Send him (her) out there for two months to call on as many people as he can in a day. Perhaps at an aggressive pace of 8 -10 appointments per week, he makes about 60-80 client meetings in 2 months. At the end of two months, he reports:

• I've made no sales
• Although many people like me
• They liked how I looked- said I was a good image for the company
• I took 10 of those people out to lunch
• 12 others asked me to call them back next month

You'd wonder – probably out loud - why you're paying this salesman $100,000 to not generate any sales.

Think of your advertising like that. That $100,000 spent in any or all media is a lot of money. You're expecting your salesman to represent you and close the sale. Why would you expect any less of your advertising?

After all, as we witnessed back in Media Spike #10 - Advertising is Salesmanship in Print. If you expect your sales rep to make a sale, why not expect the same from your ad?

It should be driving to a sale. Or be an integral part of a sales strategy. Spending $100,000 on Image to look good and deliver no new business is a very tough return on investment.

Do your ads have to be as Over the Top as Sir Elton? Probably not.
But they do have to show you've got the quality, consistently from month to month, year to year - like Mr. Elton, to get audiences coming back for more.

If you're going to invest in your company by telling everyone what you do, THEN TELL EVERYONE WHAT YOU DO. You need not be as flamboyant as some showmen - but you do need to make yourself memorable.

So memorable, that your audience wants to buy from you, again and again and again.

Stay tuned,

Media Spike # 43 – Why Are You Advertising?

Hello and welcome.

Why Advertise?

Genuinely? Why are you advertising? Shouldn't it be like actor Kevin Costner's classic movie 'Field of Dreams' in which the voice says ' If You Build It, They Will Come!

The sad reality is just putting a glitzy, or sexy or pretty ad out there doesn't turn the cash register. Your ads have to give the customer something they need to relieve pain or something that gives them pleasure.

• With the possible exception of your inventory and your payroll, advertising is often many companies largest investment. It costs so much...doesn't it?

• Interesting Dilemma!!

If it doesn't work, it's an expense, and why did you waste so much money?

If it works and delivers sales and referrals and more business, it's an investment, and you get promoted!

• So why do you do it?

Before we share our thoughts on this, let me ask you something.

What do your neighbours do for 'work'?

When they go off on their commute each day to the office or factory or wherever, what are they doing?

Do you know?
Maybe they're in marketing too. Perhaps they are computer professionals.

Maybe accountants, and financial managers.
Could be some of them specialize in recreation management while others
are professional chefs and caterers.

You're all living in the same neighbourhood and with some variations, you're all in roughly the same income bracket. But if you are making $61K per year for instance and you know what you're doing, what does your neighbour do that allows them to live in the same neighbourhood as you.

Most of us don't wear our occupations on our sleeves so you'll usually never know unless the work clothes –ie; uniform, are a giveaway.

So it's possible, no indeed probable, that someone who can solve your tax planning, fix your plumbing, do your daughter's dance lessons, is on the same bus or train with you and you don't know it.

Trouble is, that's the way too many businesses operate.

They don't tell the community – local- national- International- what it is they do and they wonder why no-one buys from them.

As you've gathered by now, my role is a Media Planner and Buyer and negotiator and strategist, and as readers who have been with me this far along, you're seeing my style day after day. So far, about an eight week interview.
(How am I doing? ….Thanks!)

So rather than pick my media services blindly out of a Newspaper or On-line promotion, you get to learn first hand, my style.

Demonstration - day by day -, a slow drip approach, builds a lot more comfort and confidence than thrusting myself at you with an IN YOUR FACE presence.
And this is what your advertising needs to do.

It needs to tell others what you do and why they should hire you or buy your product or service.

Your advertising is your lifeblood of your business. Don't ever cut the jugular because this is where your business is coming from.

So back to our opening question. Why Do You Advertise? Well……..

Here's Why to Advertise!

• **It creates store traffic:** The more people who come into your store (or know about your business) the more opportunities you have to make sales.

• **It attracts new customers:** Your market is always changing and evolving and regular advertising keeps up with them until their lifestyle meets your product.

• **It encourages repeat business:** Due to endless shopping options now, you need to work harder to build and retain loyalty.

• **It generates continuous business:** Even slow days can produce sales. You have overhead to meet and new people to reach.

• **It is an investment in success:** By keeping your message fresh in your consumers mind, you'll be the natural choice when it's time to buy.

• **It keeps you competitive:** There are only so many customers in the market ready to buy at any one time. You have to maintain a steady presence so your regular customers (and prospective ones) know you're still there or you'll lose to more aggressive competitors.

• **It projects a successful image:** Advertising tells customers and competitors that your doors are open and you are ready for business.

• **Advertising doesn't cost,...it pays!!**

Stay tuned,

Media Spike # 44 – What Did We Get For It?

Welcome - Did I ask you this already?

What did we get for it?

We spent all this money and what did we get for it?

So went the controlled rant of one client in the past 24 hours as we were reviewing last year's activities.

This is a modest but consistent client for us and one of my colleagues last year encouraged more Social Media during our last 12 month campaign.

Not necessarily a component I would have pushed so aggressively, but it was part of the schedule nonetheless. Until the day of reckoning – yesterday - when the client asked, 'We spent $24,000 on Social Media' and what did we get?'

No appreciable or measurable increase in traffic to our site, or to our health clinic. We were 'Liked' apparently 20 to 30 times, but no like ever translated to someone walking in our door. There was no increase in the call to action on the website or 1-800# to schedule an appointment.

So what did we get for it?

Tough to answer when the media can't defend itself, and lip service of saying it's Raising Awareness pales in the wake of Not Raising Sales.

To his credit, my digital colleague did tap-dance to express that it was a contributor to the overall effect of the campaign and it reached a new audience. Very true. But new or incumbent, if they ain't buying, it doesn't matter who likes you.

Happily, our Newspaper banner ads, and magazine 1/3rd page ads pulled the trigger on sales more than any other media and the spikes in business were readily identifiable as to when print media appeared.

I spoke of Social Media briefly in Media Spike #35, and again I don't want to trample this format, but believe it needs to be used differently to deliver a desired return.

My clients' $24,000 disappeared into the ether of On-line without a trace, and without a glimmer of return on investment. But they are the lucky ones as I'm certain many clients have invested substantially more dollars to come away with the same perplexed feeling.

What did we get for our money?

Dear reader, you may remember that through this series, I have touched on, I think just about all forms of media, to varying degrees.

I believe they all need to continue to be a part of the fabric of communication. Newspaper, and Radio, On-Line and Television, Outdoor and Magazines, and subsets of all of these are just more tools in our efforts to communicate.

However as more advertisers are becoming more market savvy, the demand for ROI is more and more critical. If you can't find a way to measure it, don't use it.

Stay tuned,

Media Spike # 45 – Target Acquired! Ready, Aim, ….Sell!

Greetings once again.

What's a Target Group?

Sounds like a bunch of innocent people at the wrong end of a Shooting Gallery.

In truth it may seem we are taking shots – unfairly - at our audiences wherever they are, but therein is the dilemma – Exactly *where* are they?

Not too long ago, I heard someone describe their Target Group as anyone with a credit card.

Goodness you'll have a long and expensive campaign reaching the estimated five billion credit card holders around the globe. If you can pull it off, more power to you.

Genuinely, very few products have such a global demand. And if they do, someone might already be harvesting all these consumers. Perhaps consider constructing your Target Group so you can better qualify their attributes and quantify how big a market they are.

One major Canadian client I worked with a number of years back suggested they wanted to be 'National'.

A noble sentiment. Somewhat unattainable given the scope of their budget. But it was a starting platform and allowed us to have a 'Base' audience from which we could refine our ideal target group.

An FYI (For Your Information) at this writing, the most recent Government of Canada Statistics* advise that the National population of Canada is an estimated 35,158,304. All persons, all ages- 35.1 Million.

.* Note: Population as of July 1.
·**Source:** Statistics Canada, CANSIM II, table 051-0001.   Last modified: 2013-11-22
http://www5.statcan.gc.ca/cansim/a26?lang=eng&retrLang=eng&id=0510001&tabMode=dataTable&srchLan=-1&p1=-1&p2=9

So how do you determine whom you're trying to reach?

I defined this as my Target Group Editing

•This is an arena, which your media team should be able to help you. Logically, and methodically, reducing that huge universe to a more manageable size.

•

•Some of these steps you saw already in the Spike of Angels 57 Spikes Media Planning Guide & Template by clicking here which you first downloaded when you signed up. Let's start by eliminating whom we don't want. If this can be done in bigger chunks, (Ie: we want to reach only men for this brand of Scotch product- this eliminates women and children), then you can more quickly trim your target to manageable sizes.
•**Some preliminary questions:**
•Are you targeting men or women? Both?
•What age group are you trying to influence?
•Is there a particular geography you need to cover - national, regional, provincial, local?
•Do they have the income, personal or household to support buying your product?
•Are they living in major urban centres or rural areas?
•Do you have an idea of their media habits?
Ie: typically which media in their geography are they most exposed to?

• A sample target group follows. For this client, we wanted to reach the most appropriate audience who would be interested in purchasing a **Computer Printer**

• **Sample Target Audience**: For Computer Printers (circa 1999)

From our 31 Million Canadians at that time, we edited our universe as follows:

Our primary candidate audience is defined as
A well educated Male, living in a major urban centre, who enjoys an above average income, and currently has a home computer.

Here's how we got there: This profile was created from our earlier research via PMB(Print Measurement Bureau) and NADBank which confirms the profile of the primary users of printers are:

• **Age/Sex:** Predominantly, but not exclusively male, aged 25-54. 60% of Canadian Adults 18+ are between ages of 25-54, yet they account for 85.4% of Business Computer Customers (PMB 1997)

• **Education:** University graduates account for less than 1/5th of all households. But they account for almost 1/3rd of computer ownership. • 50% of Home Computer purchasers attended University, versus 36% of adult population.

• **Own personal computer:** according to the Radio Marketing Bureau & Statistics Canada 31.6% or almost 4 Million Canadian homes - had a computer at the end of 1996. That is triple the penetration from only a decade earlier.(10.3% in 1986). Current figures show it having crested 40%.

• **Have Home Office**: and they also may operate a small business from home

• **Enjoy Mid to High Household Income:** 20% of the households with higher incomes were four times more likely to have a computer than those with incomes in the lowest 20%.

• 41.3% of Adults 18+ report incomes in excess of $50,000 but they account for 72.4% of Business Computer Customers

• **Live in major urban centres:** 39.4% live in community sizes of 1 million +, with the following top six ranking of: Toronto, Montreal, Vancouver, Ottawa/Hull, Edmonton and Calgary

Narrowing the Field

• The preceding paragraphs will demonstrate that asking and answering some realistic questions about the target group can help you focus on delivering a campaign with more efficiency, impact and memorability.

• In constructing our media recommendation, we knew our primary Target Group should be:

> Men aged 25-54, who were university graduates who had incomes in excess of $50,000 and they lived in major urban centres, predominantly in the top six markets noted above.

This streamlined our original 31 Million candidates substantially, and allowed us to select media which best reached them within our budget.

PLUS: All of this media refinement allowed our creative to work harder because we reached our candidate purchaser more strategically, and funds were not wasted on irrelevant media.

As in all media, on-line or offline, you do not have to 'buy more' to reach your customers, you just have to buy smarter.

Stay tuned,

Media Spike # 46 – It's All Your Choice

Here's a great way to start the day.

A Blank Cheque!
All the money you could ever want!
No need to hesitate on what to buy, because you can buy it all.

You can only spend it on the media, which you believe best reaches your target group.

So – **WHAT** do you choose?

It's in your court.
Nobody saying you can't afford it.
Only saying you have to rationalize and defend your choice.

So – **WHAT** do you choose?

Sometimes we clamour to have unrestricted freedom, nobody telling us what to do, no-one saying we can't pick this or that- and we get what we want. The restraints come off.

Nobody to raise a fist against. No-one quashing our desires. You have unlimited opportunity to pick whatever you'd like. But once you've made your choices, you have to defend them.

To show they are the right selections to reach and influence your audience to actually trigger a sale of product or service. You need to show a reasonable expectation of return on investment.

So - **WHAT** do you choose?

Scary isn't it? I finally get to pick what I want to pick,.....now what the heck am I going to pick? Sometimes too much choice is a dangerous thing.

Extensive food buffets always leave me feeling unsatisfied. Not leaving hungry as I've had my fill. Just unsatisfied that I couldn't eat a little bit more of everything.
If they had fewer choices, maybe I would not feel so bad about not being able to eat three platefuls.

Your media choices today can leave you feeling like that.

The litany of choices as we've seen in earlier Media Spikes is nearly endless. And subsets within tabs, within sections, within features, within just one Newspaper or Website or Magazine can have you reeling in the enormity of the task of trying to reach everyone in your target group.

This is why testing and sampling and experimenting can leave you feeling much more confident and assured of your choices. When you get to put your marketing muscle behind one or two or three tested media choices, you know you have given yourself the best opportunity to reach and influence your target group with accuracy, efficiency and – we hope- memorability.

When you choose your media blindly, and base it on a hunch or feeling, that leaves a hollow feeling in the stomach and bank account if it doesn't deliver.

Conversely if, for example, you've taken the time to test Newspaper, and Radio, and Magazine and On-line, and Outdoor, with carefully monitored tests of performance, then you'll be able to roll out the big campaign with huge comfort that you are using the best tools to impact your audience.

There are certainly never any shortages of media opportunities. Do not despair if a 'Special' feature has to come and go without you. Believe me, there will be another option - often a better choice, waiting in the wings. Very few of these are life and death, or essential 'keepers'.

Certainly if an opportunity comes up which fits the target group, and budget, and timing, and can be worked into the schedule effortlessly, then by all means embrace it.

Please do not be swayed just because it's cheap. Yes a lower price can make it attractive to you.

But if it didn't meet the target group criteria to be included before, it doesn't suddenly become a great fit just because it's cheaper. Make sure it meets the objectives and criteria of the campaign before making it a part of your strategy.

As always, the choice is yours. **So NOW – What do you choose?**

Stay tuned,

Media Spike # 47 – As Surely As The Sun Will Rise In The East

Welcome. Hope it's a good day.

Flavour of the month?

If you're around to enjoy all 12 months, that's not a bad thing.
But many campaigns are designed around a 4 or perhaps 8-week cycle and then disappear.

A huge cacophony of noise shouting 'I'm Here', 'Come Try Me Now', 'Limited Time Only', and it may or may not trigger sales, awareness, interest and then marketing flatlines.

No question the money has to be spent smartly. Efficiently. Timely and deliver results.

But your campaign should be based on specific timing, using best research for the media, which can consistently, persistently be in front of your target for as long a period as you're able.

Today I may not be in the mood to buy your hamburger, or purchase winter tires, or need that cruise vacation, or a new bicycle. BUT that does not mean your message won't work next week, or 26 days from now, or 4 months from today. Therein is the challenge for most products.

Keeping your name top of mind to an audience who may not need you at the time you're advertising.

But you need to keep enough profile in front of them so that when the time comes for them to want a hamburger, winter tires, cruise vacation or bicycle, YOU are the provider they think of.

In my experience to date, perhaps yours too, the most successful clients I've enjoyed working with had one thing in common – they advertised consistently.

Sometimes different spend levels.
Often different media mixes as we were experimenting what worked and what didn't. Very often, different products within the same family.

But they were in the marketplace on an ongoing basis. Their year might look something like: In for 3 months, out for one, in for 2 months, out for ½ month, back in for 3 months, out for one, back in for 1 ½ months.

They were never out of their marketplace long enough to be forgotten. The residual of recognition they had built up carried them through their short hiatus periods.

I grant you not every advertiser has the resources to keep consistent weight up through the year. But importantly, they maintained some presence to a primary market, and kept their message(s) out there on a reliable consistent presence.

When there is a specific seasonality or time sensitivity to your product or event or service, then it makes absolute sense to create awareness in advance of the peak sales period and sustain presence through that flight.

When your campaign is not tied to specific months of the calendar, it can be very advantageous to keep your name, product, service out there on an ongoing basis.

If you roll the dice and spend the lot on a two month campaign in March and April, you're counting on less than **20% of the year to deliver 80% of your sales** and revenue. Better be really, really sure that your two month flight can generate a year's worth of presence **and** keep you top of mind for your client in the face of all your competition for a full year until the next campaign.

This is the advertising world's embodiment of the internationally acclaimed principle sometimes called the Law of the Vital Few. You might know it better as the Pareto Principle or the 80/20 Principle.

> *In the early 1900's, Vilfredo Federico Damaso Pareto observed that in Italy at the time, 20% of the population had 80% of the wealth. This ratio could be found in multiple applications and continues to today. We witnessed this in Media Spike #19 regarding the power of headlines.*

The magnitude of this principle was pointed out to me by Mr. Jon McCulloch. Copywriter. Author. Entrepreneur. Consultant. An irascible, colourful (unabashedly vulgar - but colourful sounds tamer) dynamo, who pulls no punches, and spares no-one his vile. He is equally, at times brilliant, thoughtful, professional and supportive in spite of himself. You can learn much from him starting here . (jonmcculloch.com) Be forewarned, if you're too sensitive you won't like Jon's style- but you will learn a great deal.

It's a lot easier to sell to an existing customer than to continually generate new ones. That's why a sustained presence over the long term will build the brand and increase long-term memory of what you offer.

Do not rely on your clients to remember you. You have to make yourself unforgettable.

Stay tuned,

Media Spike # 48 – Whether It Works Or Not!!!

Thank you for coming back.

What an eye-opener!

A turn of phrase that stares you right in the face everyday, but sometimes from left field it hits you like a thunderclap.

To this point, my Media Spikes have spoken of different budget levels from $100,000 to a $Million to levels above and below that. The budgets available certainly offer you different media combinations, but one truism remains, no matter what level you're spending at, your media investment will cost you the same **whether it works or not!**

Did you get that?
Whether your campaign is successful or not, it still costs you the same.

$5,000 for two Newspaper ads.
$25,000 for a 3 weeks Radio campaign.
$55,750 for a 2 month Outdoor Poster campaign with local magazine support.
$612,350 for an integrated multi-media campaign of Radio, On-line, Newspaper, Magazines, TV, etc.

You've spent the money. Whether it works or not. You've spent it. Don't you want, at a bare minimum, to be able to recover those costs with product sales?

Certainly you hope for a substantially better return on investment than just breaking even.

But it begs the question, is just buying 'more' the answer?

More TV to reach a wider audience?
More Radio to support the Outdoor campaign?
More Magazines to give more detail and colour to the campaign?
More On-line via BigBoxes and Skyscrapers and Leaderboards and Vokens and scrolling Catfish to stay in front of the elusive websurfers?

Those are all good things. As a professional buyer, I can always spend more money smartly.

But for too many advertisers, the rush is there to buy Now, Now, Now- don't care what it takes just get it bought now. So they limit their choices by not leaving enough lead-time for planning and negotiations.

Then everything becomes last minute and they puzzle over why they don't get the choicest positions or programs or options, but are gung-ho to spend the money anyway.

In truth, I've seen clients who spend more time and energy agonizing where they'll go on vacation for a week that sets them back two grand than they will on a campaign where they'll spend six figures and not care where it goes.

Perhaps this is why I push so hard for you to use the **FREE**
Spike of Angels 57 Spikes Media Planning Guide & Template by clicking here

A special 8 page brief to help you get your ad planning started.

The key element within this document is to help you focus and drill down and as clearly as possible, identify your target group.

In Media Spike #45, we noted our real life sample to help identify our computer printer purchaser candidates. We trimmed our candidates from 31 Million to a smaller universe of well-educated males living in specific cities with a certain income level and age bracket. And that's a big enough audience to pursue.

Please, please resist the temptation to drill too deeply.

So much data.
So many numbers that could be used.

Age, gender, geography, employment, income bracket, kids in household, marital status, shoppers, savers, total assets with and without real estate, own luxury vehicles, like to golf, or play tennis, or drink tea more than coffee, buy organic dog food, are smokers – or non-smokers, play games on-line, have devoted more than 30 minutes a day to their commute, like to listen to the Radio in the car......and the list goes on, and on, and the trouble is you can get to refine your audience so tightly that:

A) It becomes too small a universe to target with any media, and becomes statistically unreliable
B) It eliminates some serious prospects from your buying list because of one too many filters
C) You put restrictions on your audience, which may not be relevant.

One of my favourites was distilling a client's universe so precisely that it ended up being targeted to:

> All Ontario males between the ages of 25 to 34, who were unmarried, had a college + education, who were working in technology fields, who were left-handed, and liked to smoke cigars when they walked their dogs!

The resulting audience size was – well to say laughable is being generous.

You are going to spend the money for your advertising and marketing.

By all means do all the testing necessary to refine your messages and media mixes.

Certainly use your research tools to help you focus your message.

But don't get so caught up that it becomes analysis paralysis.

Take the time to learn small to succeed big. Remember it will cost you the same whether the campaign works or not.

Stay tuned,

Media Spike # 49 – Who Are We Again?

Thank you for joining me again, dear reader.

We're in the home stretch. Have you enjoyed the ride?

The finish line is in sight. Including today's effort, there are nine (9) Media Spikes remaining in this inaugural series. I hope you have found it informative, helpful, provocative (?), and entertaining.

Inquiries have come from different corners about my background, my client and agency history, and what campaigns have I worked on to somehow verify my authenticity.

I've often expressed, **With any luck, you've never heard of me.**

If you don't know me, then I've done my job.

The media person isn't supposed to take centre stage, the client is.

My job is to get them on as many stages as possible so they can be seen by all the right prospects, while I'm in the shadows pulling the curtains.

I did share a few entries in the extended P.S. of Media Spike #29, complete with a few entries of campaigns you may recognize. But until now you didn't know I had anything to do with them.

However the inquiries persist so to give more credence to everything you've read from me to date, here are many of the Ad Agencies I've worked with, and a litany of clients, where, I've been privileged to be the steward of their ad budgets

AD AGENCIES

Agency 59 (Axmith McIntyre & Wicht)
Bright Red Communications
Canadian Media Corporation
Cardon Rose Inc.
Carrot Marketing
DMB&B Advertising
FPR Communications
Grey Group Canada
Langmuir Mangialardo Advertising
LMA
Lackey Communications

Larter Advertising
Media Buying Services
The Backroom Agency
The Marketing Garage
The MacDonald Kerr Partnership
Thirteen (13) AD Advertising
Method Branding
Orange Bazooka
Promotivate
Triple P Promotions
DEC Sports Marketing

CLIENTS

Automotive & Transport
Canadian Kenworth Trucks
Firestone Tire and Auto Centres
GO Transit
Mercedes Benz Canada
Suzuki Automotive
TNT Kwikasair

Clothing & Accessories
KIWI Shoe Polish
TANA Shoecare
Timberland Workboots
Young Canada Children's Clothing

Entertainment
Ontario Director's Guild
Kaneff Golf
Let's PartyTalk.com

Financial
Central Guaranty Trust
Interac
RoyNat Capital Lenders

CLIENTS

Floor Coverings
Altro Flooring
Harding Carpets
Monsanto Canada

Food Products
Chicken Farmers of Ontario
Jordan's Cereal
Pinnacle Foods

Government
Federal Government of Canada
Ontario Ministry of the Attorney General-(Drinking & Driving)
City of Toronto

Health
Clear Nail Laser Centres
CINOT- Children In Need Of Treatment (Dental)
Heart & Stroke Ontario
Great West Life Insurance

CLIENTS

Hospitality & Travel
Air Canada Vacations
Globus & Cosmos Touring
Howard Johnson & Knights Inn
Niagara On The Lake
Preferred Hotels & Resorts Worldwide
Toronto Prince Hotel
TICO-Travel Industry Council of Ontario

Humanitarian & Spiritual
The Salvation Army (Pro-Bono)
The Canadian Bible Society

Music
COSMO Music
Yamaha Canada Music

Technology
01 Communique
Canon Canada Inc.
Forminco
Pioneer Electronics
Rockwell International
Telehop

For 3 decades, you may have unknowingly witnessed my handiwork. In the majority I had nothing to do with the message you saw. But I had everything to do with you being able to see it.

Stay tuned,

P.S. While I'm on the subject of my history, you can also visit, http://www.firstimpressionsmedia.ca/do-you-ever-stop-.html, and on my site you'll see several entries of Praise from agencies and clients alike.

Media Spike # 50 – Fifty/Fifty Chance

Greetings.

Seems somehow appropriate doesn't it?

Media Spike #50 to talk about 50/50.

Many campaigns have evolved from year to year using tried and true media that consistently delivers for them. Such was the case from the insurance company I referenced in earlier Media Spikes. Only Bus Cards and Radio. But these worked. So they stayed with them.

Other campaigns seem to flit from media to media with no rhyme or reason from month to month, season to season. Consider this debate:

Is Newspaper a good contender for us? Absolutely yes, because of the local coverage and large space detail opportunity in a ½ page or larger ad.

Is Newspaper a good contender for us? Absolutely not, because it typically has a 24-hour shelf life, the colour costs are exorbitant, and other media are displacing it.

Pick a Media: Radio, Television, Newspaper, Magazine, On-Line, Social Media, Rink Boards, Coffee Cup Sleeves, Elevator Door Wraps, Taxicab Top Signs, Exterior Bus Card, Transit Shelters, Horizontal Posters, Blimps, Stairisers, and the list goes on…you can argue a case for and against any of them at any time.

Thus it's very critical that when an agency says ' This year we're recommending Radio and Magazines'… you want to understand why they're abandoning the TV and Newspaper and On-Line campaign they vociferously pitched last year.

Last year's campaign may have had muted success. But the agency should still be able to defend the recommendation.

Many factors go into the success or failure of any campaign. If it tanks, yes it could have been a poor media choice, or equally a lacklustre creative, or a natural or manmade event (Earthquakes, Princess Diana's death) may trump all advertising, no matter how compelling.

If, If, IF….you have been tracking and testing each ad in each media, you'll know empirically what is working and what isn't. This is your best barometer for, or against changes to the campaign.

I am always in favour of exploring new media. Testing different options. See what works. What can be edited out. What should be the new piece. Learn from campaign to campaign what is working.
Change what's underperforming and try something new.

For comparison, would you change over your entire wardrobe just because you get a hole in one pair of socks? Not likely. Although I would hope you'd replace the socks!

Mostly though it should be a signal to introduce something new.
As I just mentioned, you can always make a case for and against any media.
Ideally you want these based on merit and results.

Too often, media inclusion or exclusion is done on a whim, or a gut feeling, or a necessary budget surgery, when it should be based on measurable results.

As I mentioned recently, <u>you will spend the same whether the campaign works or not.</u> Why not take the time to be certain it's working before you start making wholesale changes?

Stay tuned,

PSSSSST- Hey! Over here. yes You. Come here for a minute, please.

I have a Special BONUS Just for YOU as a Reader of 57 Spikes.

It's my privilege and appreciation to offer you a complimentary copy of my Spike of Angels Media Handbook.

A twenty page guide to step by step instructions media plans for Newspaper Outdoor and Internet.

Spike of Angels

give you some to manage your Radio,

This offer is not repeated Currently not on the e-mail Not on any other

elsewhere. series. correspondence.

Media Handbook
Nowhere but through this link. Exclusive to you as a book reader as my way of saying THANK YOU for staying with me this far along.

Spike Of Angels Media Handbook
http://www.firstimpressionsmedia.ca/media-handbook-from-spike-of-angels.html

Welcome to Checkpoint Number Five

A summary of our fifth series of two weeks, and 10 more Media Spikes presented.

Let's take a look back at what we covered.

#41: Trying to decipher industry jargon. Every business has its own language of terms and abbreviations known only to the insiders of each business. Just learning Reach and Frequency and GRP's will put you miles ahead of your competition.

#42: You don't have to be a rock star like Elton John to stand out from the crowd. Just be consistent and memorable and keep showing up.

#43: Why do you advertise? You're creating store traffic. You are attracting new customers. You are encouraging repeat business. It tells people you are here with solutions for them. It keeps you competitive and it conveys a successful image. Advertising doesn't cost- It Pays!

#44: What happened to all the money? Does more good money disappear into oblivion once you use On-line ads? We hope not, but it's important to not abandon what's working just to go where all the action is. There may be a lot of activity in new media, but how much of it produces results for you?

#45: Who is your target group? The better you can define and refine who your target group is, the more focused your ads can be. The less waste you'll experience and pay for. We whittled an original audience of 31 Million Canadians to a very specific audience for computer printers. It pays to focus.

#46: So what do you choose? You have a blank cheque to run ads anywhere. Where do you want to run your ads? You finally have the chance to do anything you choose. So what do you choose?

#47: Flavour of the month? Too many campaigns have short life cycles that are expected to drive the sales for an entire year. Why? Wouldn't it be a better use of funds to have a consistent push out there all year. Maybe a couple of extra hits in seasons specific to what you do, but regular presence will sustain profile, build longer term brand recognition and keep your costs amortized over a year and not a sudden spike.

It's not always about buying more, it's about buying smarter.

#48: Whether the campaign works or not, it still costs you the same. Remember to use all the tools at your disposal to clearly identify who your target is and where they are so you spend smarter. Test small to succeed big.

#49: With any luck - you've never heard of me until now. Sharing my history of agencies and clients.

#50: You can always make a case for and against any media. The court of last resort - your customers - is the true barometer to see what works/sells, and what doesn't. Testing will separate the shell game from the sell game.

Dear Reader, can you believe it? You already have fifty days of tips, recommendations, insights and teaching to help improve your advertising. We're coming into the home stretch of seven more- HANG ON!!

Thank you for your continued interest and support. The Media Spikes will resume their standard delivery pattern. I'm so pleased to field your questions and look forward to hearing from more readers.

Thank you I look forward to hearing from you.

Stay tuned,

Media Spike # 51 – Waiting on Tables

Oh good. You've joined us once again. Perfect.

BEHAVE LIKE YOU OWN THE PLACE.

If you're relying on your advertising to have some impact, to make some noise, raise the awareness of who you are and what you do, then **BE BOLD,** and **TAKE OVER THE SPACE WITH ABSOLUTE DOMINANCE.**

Sure smart guy. Mr. Media here thinks I'm made of money. Only clients with deep pockets can do that.

Well if you're too gunshy about smart, powerful, intrusive advertising, then this strategy may not appeal to you. However, I applaud this thinking by a modest jewelry store in a mid-size mall I recently ventured into.

My lovely bride and I recently became first time grandparents. As a keepsake for the occasion, she checked several jewelers in the mall, looking for just the perfect piece to add to an existing bracelet.

We took a break from this expedition and headed to the foodcourt.

Once settled, I began to notice my table top, then the one beside me, and the three beyond that and then the impact hit me like a thunderclap.

In a confined space of the foodcourt, on nearly 100 tables, was a circular decal, nearly covering the entire tabletop.

Every one of them bore the same logo of one of the very same jewelers we had been in. Not only did they OWN every table, reaching every pair of eyeballs, IN ADDITION they had the foresight to provide 8 to 10 different looks so patrons could look at the store inventory to help them choose, before going into that same store in the mall.

Just brilliant.

They had the werewithal to utilize Place Based Marketing, waiting for their target audience to arrive, and when they did come to the Food Court, there was no way of avoiding the message if you were a patron there.

It reinforced their image. It targeted candidates who were already in the same mall. It did not get buried among other Newspaper ads. It gave a variety of messages. It offered appeal to multiple audiences with a buffet of jewelry selection options, and it also included 3 calls to action:

• Showing their location in the mall relative to the foodcourt,
• It listed a Phone number (cell phone users, everyone!!) and
• It listed their website for further exploratory at a later date by the patrons

Smart, tactical, efficient, memorable OWNERSHIP of the tabletops created an impression on this writer and I'm sure on thousands of other patrons of all ages.

This is just one example of a client using opportunities within reach. They may have supported this with other media placements I'm unaware of. However, I left that Mall remembering only one Jeweler.

As fates would have it, I did patronize their same store in another city soon after. The residual impact of that Foodcourt presence made the difference for staying Top of Mind.

And they did this by staying on Top of Tables.

Stay tuned,

Media Spike # 52 – Paging Your Customer! Paging Your Customer!

Welcome. Hoping it's a great day whenever you're reading this.

So what's the best choice?
Excuse me?

Dennis with all these media options that have been swirling these past ten weeks or so, there MUST be a best in all that.

Earlier in my career, I may have jumped at that to say you MUST use, blah blah blah blah, or else the campaign won't be effective.

The ever-changing landscape means that all these providers have their place.
They all work to varying degrees. Sometimes spectacularly well.
Other times dismal failures.

This is why I come back to our earlier mantra of Testing. And Testing. And Learning. And Testing.

Some will call it practice. Others regard it as ongoing vigilance of a client's (or their own) budget.

Keep trying, to see what's working. When it works, keep trying to improve it.
When it's working to your satisfaction, put your media muscle behind it.

Yeah, yeah Dennis. Wonderfully philosophical and poetic, but what's the best one for me?

The answer to that is kinda why I get paid. To discover what's working and to make it work harder.

As for which media is best. All of them. None of them. I am convinced the best campaigns are those which use the strengths of multiple media to be in front of their candidate audiences as efficiently and effectively as possible.

That combination will be unique to each advertiser and as aggressive or modest as their budgets and nerves allow.

Our Closing Spikes in this series will speak to strengths and limitations of several media, and my thoughts on how to best use them. Today we'll start with

Magazines

- Magazines command the readers' attention. The reader is much more likely to be engaged with their magazine(s) of choice without the distraction of other media.

- Magazine advertising gives you the opportunity for more persuasive storytelling and detail and a deeper connection with the reader.

- The multitude of Magazines appealing to specific niches allow your messaging to be very targeted and focused on specific interests of your audience.

- You can customize your ad from issue to issue, or magazine to magazine to test content, and measure response to different appeals.

- Magazines are a trusted friend you invite into your world, on your time. And you can go back to it multiple times after purchasing only one copy, and refer to it as long as you like.

- Multiple studies have confirmed that increased Magazine advertising in the media mix will improve the overall ROI (Return on Investment) across a diverse range of product categories.

- Face it - Magazine advertising sells. Magazines are often cited as the key driver in the purchase cycle, providing the stimulus for readers to act on the ads they see.

The more specific the niche, the more the readers are self-qualifying. You won't buy or subscribe to Golfers Go To Guide, for example, unless you're an avid golfer. If you're selling to the golf industry, it's perfect targeting and an efficient use of dollars with minimal wastage.

Magazines offer a tactile experience, which no other non-print media offers. Even reading them 'On-line', while efficient, is unlike turning the pages of a crisp, colourful entrancing magazine filled with glittering editorial and robust photography.

So when you're ready to use Magazines, **please remember:**

• Colour ads always enjoy better readership (and we expect memorability), than Black & White ads

• Larger ads enjoy better readership than smaller ads. Try to use a Full Page as well as your budget will allow.

• If you can get them without paying a premium, choose a Cover position. Or negotiate for it. ie: In the next year, we will bring a schedule of six, full page 4 colour magazine ads to your magazine. During the course of that schedule, we'd like a minimum of two of these to be cover positions at the regular page rate.

• Use good creative. Keep testing to find what works. The long-term impact can't be overstated as you are creating your image, and want to be seen as someone your customers would like to be seen with.

• Always negotiate for best rates. Don't go in with all guns blazing, but if you're prepared to be in multiple editions of a magazine, they should come back to you with an attractive rate and or other value added opportunities.

> Ie: Bonus distribution of the magazine at a trade show you are part of.
> A complimentary Reader Reply Card.
> Be part of the Magazines measurement study (Starch).
> Perhaps complimentary distrbution of your literature to their database via e-mail/mailing/newsletter.

• BE MEMORABLE – Goodness, you've paid a LOT of good money to get in front of these people.

Don't be lost at the turn of a page. Magazines deliver **STOPPING POWER**. Use it.

Stay tuned,

P.S. Nothing thrills me like a good story. It all starts with the letters. You will find a library of stories and information
 at: http://www.Magazinescanada.ca/home

If you did not get a chance to take a peek earlier, here's the link again to my Magazine commentary available on my website:
http://www.firstimpressionsmedia.ca/media-library-and-articles--free-.html

Media Spike # 53 - Make Waves With Airwaves

Welcome.

Does this sound familiar?

**Late night Radio/Take It everywhere I go/
My best friend when I'm lonely/ Is my late night Radio!**

And this stanza, from the late musician, John Denver, speaks volumes about the power, the portability, the intimacy and the friendship that Radio delivers. One reader expressed to me that not only is it my commuter companion, it delivers the songs that connect me to the past and to my present. So let's take today to talk about **Radio.**

Not tactile like the Magazine readership experience, but no less intrusive as an audio experience.

Among the best sales pitches to me - (as a buyer I get a lot of them) – came several years ago when the seller said please remember, <u>On the Radio, I don't have to see your product to sell it.</u>

The power of imagination by your listeners will paint the necessary backdrop. You may remember, that a little more than eight weeks ago, at the end of Media Spike #9, I spoke of Theatre of the Mind. That is the sticking point for all audio messages. The skill of the writer, without benefit of visual or graphics assistance, must establish the setting quickly, engage your attention, and deliver the message such that you remember it and act on it, long after the spot is done.

One writer, Mr. Paul Suggett – Creative Director at Digital Starz Entertainment in Englewood, Colorado likened it to an **Unlimited Special-Effects Budget.** You can create any setting you want. The listener does all the work. Creating the scene in their own mind. You don't need a host of visual clues and sets and action- the listener is doing all that from the words of your commercial.

And if you can make it humourous, that will be even better.

Thousand of comedians made their mark on Radio through the years. Long before TV, and the Internet. That capacity to entertain and create scenarios was not lost on smart advertisers who used this power of imagination to educate, inform and entertain audiences. These audiences were much more inclined to purchase from the advertisers who delivered this kind of experience.

I will ask you to please be careful of the potential distraction of sound effects in your ad. More than once I've pulled to the right hand side of the road to let an emergency vehicle pass, only to be angered it was siren used as a sound effect in a Radio ad. Engage your listeners - do not enrage them.

If you've ever wrestled with using Radio as a component to your media mix, we offer these guideposts:

• Radio Builds Top of Mind Awareness – Delivering high, affordable frequency to your audience.

• Radio is extremely portable - Considered the anytime anywhere media, Radio is with them while they are doing something else.

• Radio targets: By Station format
By Lifestyle
By Time of Day
By Environment
By Market or Geography

• Radio is a powerful stand-alone media and a perfect team player with other media in your mix
• Radio is consistent all year round
• Radio is often the lifeline of your community, and THE source of local news, weather, traffic, school closings, and special events
• Radio is My Audio Newspaper (thank you Pat G. for that excellent description)
• For those of you wondering - yes Radio and the Internet can co-exist. Indeed nearly 1/3rd of Canadian adults report they have the Radio on while they are On-line. And they report that Radio ads have often driven them to the advertisers website.

• For those who are dollar conscious: Radio delivers more audience for the same budget than most, if not all other media.

• Lastly - for now - the Radio is often the last messaging opportunity before listeners leave the car for a shopping experience. The closer you can have the message to the cash register, the greater the chance of influencing the purchase.

So What Can You Do To Improve Radio In Your Campaign?

• Take the time to get as clear as possible on identifying your target group. (and NO - not everybody with a Credit Card)
• Their geography, age, gender, income, education, hobbies, marital status, children in household etc.

• As well as you're able - and this should be easy in your local city - LISTEN to all the Radio stations. Not just YOUR favourite, but all the stations to gain a feel for their flavour, style, format, personalities.

This is time well spent. Some years back there was a prominent station I was all set to have my client appear on. However, the morning show personalities crossed the line of vulgarity a few too many times for my liking and I won't embarrass my clients by having their ads appear in that environment. I moved those ad dollars elsewhere. It just saves enormous grief.

This will help you from a comfort level where your message should be delivered and how it should be constructed to reflect the profile of the listeners of that station.   Your tonality should be adjusted to fit the station to gain greater acceptance by the listener, and not be a jarring tune out.

• Contact several Radio stations, and tell them your objectives.
    Who you are trying to reach?
    What you want to happen as a result of airing the ads.
    Do you want them to?
            Visit your store or website to make a purchase?
            Raise awareness of your service?
            Drive them to an upcoming event?
            Rally behind a candidate?

• Contact them to present a proposal to you, which gives you a reach plan presence across the station.

When you're ready, look to see if there is a sponsorship opportunity.
Above all, do not commit to a long-term schedule until you've seen and tested and measured how your campaign is performing.

• Please compose your ad so that you can track its performance. Some identifier that tells you any response could only be attributable to that ad. This will pay off in spades later in this campaign and others in the future.

• When Radio is utilized properly, it can provide an impressive Return on Investment for the advertiser.

• Money: How much are you prepared to spend to win a new customer? Not just how much are you prepared to lose if this campaign doesn't work. But how much are you ready to invest in your marketing to get a lifetime customer. (That's a grander question for all marketing.)

So – genuinely - how much are you prepared to invest in the next Radio campaign?

Don't spread yourself too thin starting out. Pick one station - maybe two, and test your ads with a call to action and see where your best responses come from.
And keep testing with other stations until you get the one(s) that provide the best results for you. It's time and money well spent.

• Radio allows you to stay Top Of Mind by going in through the ears.

Stay tuned,

P.S. Radio has been with the globe for over a century. Broadcasting triumph and tragedy, from the Beatles to Beyonce, from the car to the garden, it is ubiquitous.

While there is no end to the possibilities and the styling of how to use Radio, we thought you might like access to the former Radio Marketing Bureau's contributions. The bureau is no longer active, but the site remains as a wonderful reference tool: http://Radiomarketingbureau.ca/

In addition, you will find our Ten Part Series on Radio with a click here: http://www.firstimpressionsmedia.ca/how-to-improve-your-advertising-using-Radio---a-10-part-series.html

Media Spike # 54 – Channel Your Customer

Welcome once again.

Hope the day has dawned bright and sunny wherever you're reading this.

In the past 72 hours, I've had one client who waffled about the daunting cost of a combined Radio & TV campaign at a quarter million dollars, evolve to wanting to champion a new campaign of TV only at more than double this investment.

What is it about **Television** that still seems to trump all other players?

Well let's take a look at the lure and allure of the iconic 'boob tube'.

In Media Spike #16, I was asking if you're a fan of TV, and in Media Spike # 21 I was referencing TV as the Driver off the tee, to pursue the golf analogy, plus in Media Spike # 26 I spoke to TV's incubation in 1927 and reaching commercial birth in 1947.

I mention these previous efforts to show that despite the naysayers, Television is alive and well and living in your home. You'll find it in your living room, maybe the media room and then I'll bet you there is a screen in your bedroom and maybe one for each of the kids too?

Yes it is now on your computer, and handhelds, and tablets and at the cottage, probably on the boat too. Our thirst is unquenchable.

Perhaps moreso than any other media, Television has to continually refresh and reinvent itself.

Whether you like any of the content on all 132 channels* is up to you. But the mere presence of that kind of TV universe (* and probably more) is testament to its enormous staying power.

Its immense footprint as a persuasive platform make it irresistible to many deep pocketed advertisers, who reap the benefit of its enormous reach. Such reach and influence comes at a price. A price that many advertisers are prepared to spend to put themselves in front of millions of candidates every day.

Television brings, audio, and video in the same experience. Motion, light, sound, and demonstration, Television brings the world to any and all of your rooms that house your TV's.

Because it's in front of us all the time, it's easy to get complacent about it, but the technology that brings images from around the globe to our eyeballs in fractions of seconds is truly staggering and magic.

It's hard to not be tempted to be a part of that. I think that's why this particular project had the client salivating. The prospect of being on Television, to a huge pool of candidates (provincial at 5 Million plus) was hard to ignore. The jury is still out on whether this will be the course of action, but the prospect of showing off is enticing.
(Since the original writing, this TV campaign aired and did amazingly well, overachieving audience by 114%)

Showmanship is always exciting when delivered with the necessary panache. **Television** can do that.

• Television continues to deliver unmatched mass reach.

• Despite rumours to the contrary, consumers still spend more time with Television each day than they do with any other media.

• TV continues to be The Screen of Choice, and is considered the most persuasive and most exciting media to be a part of.

• It is not an either/or environment, but one of coexistence where TV is the ultimate Stand Alone media, as well as being a team player supporting any and all other media with targeted, extensive audio and visual muscle.

• If you've wondered about the appeal outside the home - pop in to any sports bar where multiple Television screens large and small dominate wall space or take control of our eyeballs while being perched on suspended cradles. A panorama of hockey, football, golf, tennis, curling, car racing, baseball, horse racing, boxing, and wrestling compete for attention for hours on end.

• This entire 57 Media Spikes series could have been devoted to TV and still not have had enough space.

• We have and continue to advocate Testing. TV can be an expensive arena to do that. It's why advertisers in my experience, come to 'graduate' to television. Once testing and learning has been done on a small scale, then the successes can be rolled out to bigger and wider audiences, confident they have a greater chance of success. Television sends a message to your prospects that you are successful and serious, and worth paying attention to.

• The greatest challenge for most advertisers is the cost of TV advertising. As scary expensive as it is – you'll remember my reference to one spot was whopping $77,500, in Media Spike #16, - television continues to be among the most efficient media available. Not unlike most media, you have to shop and negotiate for the best value, but dollar for dollar, you'll get excellent value for your TV dollar.

• Make your TV ad work very hard for you.

• Buy the airtime smartly. The better you can target your audience by age, gender, geography, income, education etc., the better your programming selection can be, the more targeted your buy, the better the efficiency, the more mileage you get from your budget.

• Select or recommend the type of programming you'd like to be associated with.
(IE: More comedy and drama and less reality TV, more sports and less news, more afternoon talk shows and less sports, only the dinner window of 4.30pm to 6.30pm, and after 11pm)

• You will in all likelihood, need a variety of programming to reach your audience. But I've found using a few well-chosen anchors of consistent programming in a schedule makes for more memorability than being everywhere for the sake of it.

• Don't dismiss cable TV programming as it delivers enormous penetration and can often improve your efficiencies by consistent performance. **As Tom Cruise voices in the 1993 movie, 'The Firm' about getting the other bad guys with mail fraud: 'It's not sexy, but it's got teeth.'** Cable may not have glamour written all over it, but it works.

• Keep your expectations in check with real, measurable, objectives. This is true of all media, but especially TV. The expense devoted to it means we expect instant sales and salvation.

• As I expressed in our very first meeting of Media Spike #1, Don't **Ever** give away a time at bat.

• TV means you're 'On Stage' performing. Don't miss this chance to shine.

Stay tuned,

P.S.: If you're inclined for more detail on many aspects of television, the **Television Bureau of Canada** is an invaluable resource to draw on. You can reach them here: http://www.tvb.ca/pages/home

Media Spike # 55 –SocialEyes Your Advertising?

Thanks for joining us again. Sit down anywhere - we're about to get started.

The Revolution is **HERE!**

Maybe you'll recall we visited with Chicken Little way back on Media Spike #26 about the explosion of Social Media Channels and how we have to revise our lives around it.

Not too long after that in Media Spike #35, we posed the question if Social Media is truly the advertising saviour that 'they' say it is. The debate continues.

Social Media in many of its channels, offer immediacy, engagement, relationship building, one to one exchange with interested customers, and can deliver thousands upon thousands of impressions and awareness building without costing a cent.*

You can buy based on Cost Per Click. (CPC) Cool. But if no-one clicks, what's been the value in even creating the creative? Impressions without action are still no sale. (* don't be fooled about alleged FREE on Social Media. It still costs you in time to create and or maintain presence there. No charge exposure is nice, but you still paid in other currency to be there.)

At this writing, some of the most prominent Social Media platforms include, but are not limited to:

Platform	Registered Users	Alexa Ranking
FourSquare	20 Million	#817
Facebook	1 Billion	#2
Google+	500 Million	N/A
Linked In	200 Million	#12
Pinterest	70 Million	N/A
Stumble Upon	20 Million	#146
Twitter	93.8 Million	#8

Goodness if ever you wanted choice, you can get lost in the buffet of options in Social Media alone.

Their combined connectivity is staggering with worldwide communication with friends, family, businesses, clients, new clients in the millions every day.

Are they all On-Line? Of course.
Are they all buying something? Well the jury I believe remains divided from what I can ascertain.

Several services have been diligently working to monetize their platform with mixed or sometimes very dismal returns.

In fairness, some platforms have done exceedingly well by advertisers who have taken the time to learn the nuances specific to each platform.

At this juncture, I would concur with Mr. Joey Ambrose of Joey@GoWebSolutions.com , in Tucson, Arizona who comments on the merits of Facebook advertising this way from Monday November 4th, 2013: *I think it's like any platform: You get what you put into it ie: creativity and targeting, and 2. You test, refine, wash and repeat. We've had great results with Facebook advertising, but it's not for every advertiser, and you have to measure it.*

How perfect. Even in this Digital Universe, the best way to find out if it's working is….TEST IT.

How boring is that mantra? Test It.

The media options, paper, airwaves, electrons, are simply the tools we use to distribute the message.

Want to know which one is working best? Test it. (Just like we said way back in Media Spike #14 - about 8 weeks ago now) In testing there is no failure, there is only results.

On-line is now among the fastest ways in which to do the necessary trials and testing to see what works.

Can these platforms truly be money producers for you? Perhaps. But it seems to me at this stage that with Social Media you have to constantly work hard on your ads, rather than your ads working hard for you.

Stay tuned,

Media Spike # 56 – Blow The Doors Off Using Outdoor

Glad you could join us.

On the road again?

If your first reaction to this is Willie Nelson then that's a great testament to an iconic musician and someone who has toured the world one mile at a time, by bus.

Imagine the places he's been, the venues he's played, the things he's seen, the billboards he's passed, …..?

Billboards he's passed?

We remain a nation, perhaps a continent perpetually on the go. Toing and froing. To the office or jobsite, home, shopping, traveling, visiting, always behind the wheel. Our attention and focus should always be on our driving. But the pace or lack off sometimes, plays favourably into an advertiser's strategy.

Outdoor advertising in the form of Outdoor Posters, Billboards, Transit Shelters, Wall Murals, Bus Wraps, Train Wraps, TaxiTops and Taxiwheel advertising, Truck side and Truck Top advertising, Underground Pathway electronic signage, Stadium or Arena Advertising Spaces are omnipresent and powerful.

The on the road, out of home messages can hit like a sledgehammer when a bold idea is served up in a, skyline dominating powerful visual, with just the right words. The visual impact and stopping power with brevity will resonate long after you've driven past if done correctly.

Some have likened Outdoor advertising to cheap television. You still have a powerful visual, but no audio to amplify the message. Thus the skill of your copywriter has to distill paragraphs of sales copy into a short memorable thought.

Here's an example of the power of Outdoor and the limitation of Social Media.

One client had a series of spectacular beauty shots of their wine region prepared. Each one featured a distinctive image of the region. The one word describing it all was: **untweetable.**

(Client is Wine Country Ontario, in a campaign composed by Agency 59 of Toronto, Ontario, Canada. Creative Director Mr. Brian Howlett)

How powerful is that? You have to be here to experience the vibrancy, the exquisite charm, the joy, the history, the nature, the elegance, the people, the passion, the architecture, the food, and the ambiance. A picture was certainly worth more than a thousand words, and 140 characters.

My favourite description of Outdoor Advertising is to

Make Some Noise Without A Sound

A few things to consider:

• Most Outdoor media will rotate in 4-week cycles. This way every advertiser gets exposure to multiple geography of the city(ies) where they're appearing.

• It's a chance for you to refresh or change the creative, or to ensure the same look now appears at different parts of the city.

• To the best of your ability, try to keep the media units constant from market to market. Production-wise, it's typically cheaper to print 100 paper posters at 10 feet X 20 feet size, than it is to print 65 Posters and 35 Transit Shelters.
We respect that sometimes the availabilities or not of some formats in your markets make it mandatory to use a secondary format. We'd encourage you to confirm availabilities ahead of printing to make sure you get the best value.

• Many Transit Shelters offer an excellent opportunity to remain Backlit, adding a dimension of visibility and creative 'pop' when viewed at night. This lighting is accomplished sometimes by electricity, others by battery, still others by solar lighting. Knowing this can help your production team set the colours best in your ad to maximize impact and visibility.

I have no pretensions of being a production person, but a colleague who is speaks of the impact being attributable to the substrate (paper/vinyl) and the opacity or translucence which allows more or less light to surround the image.

• Be UNMISSABLE. As I expressed recently in Media Spike #51, Behave Like You Own The Place. Dabbling, trying out, testing, experimenting is best left to less expensive media. Go Out There and Blow the Doors off Outdoors.

• I want you to get to the end of the flight feeling – WOW. We were EVERYWHERE. And if you put a call to action in the ad, your results will tell you just how much impact going Outside had.

• Apart from an explosive display of creative excellence, Outdoor offers repetition that delivers the necessary frequency for you to become memorable in a short period of time. We are creatures of habit and those habits include our driving and commuting patterns and while the media is static, the audience isn't.

• Outdoor, not unlike TV or Radio, can act very powerfully as a Stand Alone media, and many successful campaigns have relied on an Outdoor advertising campaign exclusively to be their brand builders.

* Happily, also like TV and Radio, it's a great team player via visual impact and in your face presence. It's also a wonderful tool in your arsenal as it quickly adds so many more touchpoints of communication for your message.

Has Willie Nelson seen all your ads? Well I wouldn't bet the ranch on it just yet. However, considering the mileage he's racked up touring, the Outdoor ads may be the reason he just can't wait to get on the road again.

Stay tuned,

P.S. I know you're busy. Thanks for making it this far. In case you've missed the original link from Media Spike #24, here's where you can find more Outdoor Advertising info for your reference

http://www.firstimpressionsmedia.ca/how-to-improve-your-advertising-using-Outdoor-media---a-10-part-series.html

In addition, there is also a single page, printed two sides PDF which speaks to the Powerful Partner that is Outdoor:

http://www.firstimpressionsmedia.ca/media-library-and-articles--free-.html

Media Spike # 57 – This Is Where I Came In

Greetings once again.

The most amazing part of this advertising series is that after 56 previous Media Spikes, **YOU ARE HERE!**

Not unlike how we opened this series 11 weeks ago (Presumably less if you've read the book version).

I am the lucky recipient of your eyeballs and attention for 57 consecutive business days. For those wondering or counting, this series will conclude at approximately 44,000 words. I am honoured and humbled you've stayed with me. Thank you.
The intention throughout this series was to demonstrate for you the power of owning your platform.

We've together explored, Television and Magazines, On-line/Social Media, Outdoor Media and Newspapers as well as Radio and I've offered strategy, critiques, commentary and I hope some education for you.

Clearly more than I could ever deliver in a typical 20-minute boardroom setting with each of you, this book has been my platform. A chance for you to see and experience my style first hand.

I appreciate and have enjoyed the e-mails I've received from several of you along the journey. Please keep them coming, I'm glad to help you where and when I can. Some readers may love me and want to hire as several already have. (Thank you). Others may be less passionate about my overtures and they certainly have that right.

Other readers have taken it upon themselves to access several of the links provided for further information and still others have accessed our link for our Nine Secrets E-Book in PDF Format.

In this we provide details on 9 Secrets and seven easy to follow assignments to help you improve your advertising. One reader coined it 'His Desktop Media Director' which I thought very appropriate.

It distills 30 years of being in the media trenches into 9 Secrets which you can unlock for just $30. Not bad. A buck a year for you to learn what it took me 3 decades. Lucky you.

http://www.firstimpressionsmedia.ca/online-store--start-with-9-secrets---.html

By the time you reach this page you will have made some decisions about your media, and about me.

Your reading this is testament to your interest and appreciation of my efforts to date. My fondest hope is that my words have been worth the investment of your time.

The following invitation is extended only to those who have stayed with me to now. This is an opportunity to join my Spike of Angels Inner Circle extended exclusively to readers who have stayed with me all this time.

One privilege of reading the book is you get to the front of the line for the Inner Circle more than two months faster than readers who opted for daily subscription.

At the time of this writing, there is no charge for this membership, but if that changes, we will give full up front notice of any monetary obligation, so you can make an informed decision.

The best part about continuing education is you continue learning, for as long as you choose. I do hope you will continue to be part of my e-mail universe. I've loved having you and hope I've been able to help solve one or more media problems or concerns since you've joined us.

Like you, I'm not ready to pick out curtains, but I've enjoyed our dance, dating, repartee, and the Inner Circle will bring you my continued media thinking as well as some special Bonuses and unannounced Opportunities exclusive to the Spike of Angels Inner Circle. You don't get access unless you've completed 57 Media Spikes.

Thank you it has been my privilege.

Look forward to seeing you on the Inside of the Spike of Angels Inner Circle

Sincerely,

Dennis Kelly

Welcome To Checkpoint Number Six

Number six in our series of six and the final summary of 57 Media Spikes.

Whew - you can exhale now. Thanks for staying along for the ride. Including these checkpoint summaries, you've been with me for 63 messages. About 6 months along now (maybe less if you've had the book version). I hope you've enjoyed and have been able to use some of the tips and ideas in your business practice to improve your business.

#51: Waiting on Tables. Powerful place based marketing by one enterprising jeweller gave them a big creative footprint that literally put their catalogue in the foodcourt. Top of Mind from Top Of Table.

#52: What's the best media? WELL- let me ask you....What do you want to do? Who do you want to reach? How much can you afford to spend? What do you want to say? Every campaign has -or should- have their own media mix. And Magazines, well they are a perfect place to be a good storyteller.

#53: Radio - the music is the bridge that connects my past to my present. Radio is always theatre of the mind because the listener is painting the special effects in their own mind from the narrative you provide. We also gave you a link to our 10 part series on Radio by clicking here:
http://www.firstimpressionsmedia.ca/how-to-improve-your-advertising-using-radio---a-10-part-series.html

#54: Television advertising is alive and well and living in your living room, basement, bedroom, kitchen, garage, handheld, laptop and our thirst for it is unquenchable. When you're advertising, TV means you are on stage performing. Don't miss your chance to shine.

#55: While Social Media is gaining traction and usage, it remains a sociable environment, and less-so a sales environment. But like all other media, it is evolving to find ways to monetize itself. Right now it seems you need to work very hard to make your ads work, rather than your ads working hard for you.

#56: On The Road Again with Willie Nelson and the thousands of billboards he's seen in a lifetime of touring. Outdoor media is your chance to Make Some Noise Without a Sound. We also provided a link to our 10 part series on Outdoor Media by clicking here:
http://www.firstimpressionsmedia.ca/how-to-improve-your-advertising-using-Outdoor-media---a-10-part-series.html

#57: You are HERE! Just like our series opened. We've explored lots of media options, history and links to multiple sources that I hope were worth the price of admission - Your name and E-Mail address was worth it to me.

It's been fabulous for me to have you on board. We closed out with one more link to our Nine Secrets pdf
http://www.firstimpressionsmedia.ca/online-store--start-with-9-secrets---.html

The 57 Media Spikes has reached its conclusion, but also come to a transition to the Inner Circle if you'd like to continue to receive additional media commentary.

Thank you. I look forward to seeing you as part of the Spike of Angels Inner Circle

It has been my privilege. Thank you. Be well.

Sincerely

Dennis Kelly

ADDITIONAL RESOURCES AND LINKS AVAILABLE

Mr. Chris Cardell
http://www.cardellmedia.com/marketing-testing.html

Spike of Angels Media Briefing Template
Spike of Angels 57 Spikes Media Planning Guide & Template by clicking here

http://www.firstimpressionsmedia.ca/57-spikes-planning-guide.html

Mr. Andy Owen
http://www.andyowencopyandcreative.com/

Mr. Jon McCulloch
www.jonmcculloch.com

My Blog: The Spike of Angels. – The Power of 26
http://www.firstimpressionsmedia.ca/the-spike-of-angels-blog.html

Miss Mary Ellen Tribby
http://maryellentribby.com/stop-focusing-on-one-channel-of-marketing-at-a-time/

Miss Wendy Weiss, the Queen of Cold Calling
http://www.coldcallingresults.com/

Spike Of Angels Media Handbook
http://www.firstimpressionsmedia.ca/media-handbook-from-spike-of-angels.html

Spike of Angels Inner Circle Spike of Angels Inner Circle
http://forms.aweber.com/form/42/1154807542.htm

Additionally I am pleased to share that the cover of this book as well as that of the
Media Briefing Template, and 9 Secrets of How To Improve Your Advertising, as well
as the First Impressions Media logo and assorted Spike of Angels logos, are all the
handiwork of my immensely talented colleague Mr. Angus Brimacombe of 13 AD.
http://www.thirteenad.com/   He's very good isn't he?

About The Author

Dennis Kelly is Founder and President of First Impressions Media. A Canadian independent media planning and buying advertising agency.

He is a seasoned media planner, media buyer, media director, media strategist, consultant, speaker, avid golfer and so-so mechanic.

He has been a trusted steward of dozens of clients with advertising budgets ranging from $10,000 to $4 Million.

His versatility at wearing many industry hats have made him a prized ally to clients seeking smart, responsible, creative, effective and efficient investments of their advertising budgets.

He maintains his mantra that

It's Your Advertising. Make it Well Planned and Well Spent.

His skills have been tempered in the multi-media furnaces of Television and Radio and On-Line and Outdoor and Magazines and Newspapers, planning and negotiation, and he emerged battle hardened, and dedicated to squeezing every ounce of value for every advertising dollar.

He has implemented short and long, integrated and stand-alone campaigns for entities in fields including, financial services, insurance, commuter train services, automobiles, automotive aftermarket products, beer and spirits, television manufacturers, charitable endeavours, hotels, florists, golf courses, laser medical services, footwear, clothing, footwear protection, floorcovering, music and cameras and computer printers, technology and travel services.

He remains an active member, and is a Past President of Ajax Pickering Toastmasters.

His attention to detail earned him an enviable title from an industry counterpart as being A Professional To His Fingertips.

www.firstimpressionsmedia.ca

e-mail: dennis@firstimpressionsmedia.ca

FIRST
IMPRESSIONS
MEDIA
Your Advertising.
Well Planned. Well Spent.

FIRSTIMPRESSIONSMEDIA.CA

www.ingramcontent.com/pod-product-compliance
Lightning Source LLC
Chambersburg PA
CBHW051915170526
45168CB00001B/396